THE POWER OF PERSUASION

PERSUASION

Mastering the Art of Influence

RAE A. STONEHOUSE

Live For Excellence Productions

COPYRIGHT

Ebook: ISBN: 978-1-998813-26-1

Paperback: ISBN: 978-1-998813-27-8

Audio: ISBN: 978-1-998813-28-5

INTRODUCTION

There probably isn't a day go by where we aren't exposed to the act of persuasion. Either somebody is trying to sell us something, advertising is everywhere, or we are trying to convince another to take our advice or to give us something that we want.

We developed our skills of persuasion when we were children. I recall trying to convince my parents why I should be allowed to stay up past my regular bedtime to watch a television show I wanted to see. Or why I should be able to watch a show, I was interested in that was on at the same time as a show they were watching. I'm dating myself with that example. This was back in the olden days when households had only one television. I know... it is hard to believe that people actually lived in those conditions! Even negotiating with our mothers for an extra serving of dessert or a treat helped us hone those skills of persuasion that would become so important to us in adulthood and in our careers.

This book results from the research I undertook to prepare for a presentation titled: '**The Power of Influence: Speaking to Make Things Happen!**' Ironically, as I researched the topic, I found that perhaps the presentation should have been titled '**The Power of**

Persuasion: Speaking to Get Other People to Make Things Happen!'

Nichole De Falco in her Saying What You Mean Blog, October 29, 2009, **Influence vs Persuasion: A Critical Distinction for Leaders** and those that responded to her online, provides interesting insights into the topic.

"From a purely semantic point of view, it's not such a big deal to use these terms [i.e., influence/persuasion] interchangeably. From a leadership perspective, however, the distinction can be the difference between your team carrying you on their shoulders after a victory or having them stuff you in a locker before practice."

De Falco defines **persuasion** as ... "presenting a case in such a way as to sway the opinion of others, make people believe certain information, or motivate a decision."

She provides these examples of activities that would be associated with *persuasion*:

1. Choosing words and phrases to communicate ideas that strike a responsive chord in a target audience.
2. Using a decision-matrix to steer a conversation through a path of predictable choices.
3. Orchestrating environmental conditions in which to interact with others to optimize the likelihood of a desirable outcome.

She provides the following definition of *influence*: "Influence is having a vision of the optimum outcome for a situation or organization and then, without using force or coercion, motivating people to work together toward making the vision a reality." And these activities as examples of influence in action:

- Socializing ideas to bring all the issues to light and earn buy-in.
- Giving others a voice in the decision-making process.
- Brokering meaningful relationships between unconnected groups.

- Giving others credit.
- Maintaining a track record of consistent success in a particular area.

John Smith, in his comments, provided... "persuasion" seems more about direct action in a specific situation than "influence", which seems to be concerned with overall guidance and direction.

Brian Hearn commented... "I like to say influence is about **PEOPLE —Powerful Everyday Opportunities to Persuade** that are **Lasting and Ethical**. I use the terms *influence* and *persuasion* interchangeably, but I see your point. If you are correct, then influence, or being influential, is more than just saying the right thing. It's about who you are, everything about you, which causes people to follow you. Celebrities are a good example because they can be influential despite lacking persuasive skills. By virtue of who they are, people want to be with them, like them, and do what they do."

Doug Edgar commented... "I hadn't given much thought to the distinction between persuasion and influence in a leadership context, but now that you've pointed it out, I can see a clear difference between the two. Whereas persuasion can be effectively used by anyone with a good enough story to tell, influence can be used only by leaders. Influence is one of the defining attributes of leaders. Great leaders seldom need to *persuade*, they need only *explain*."

TECHNIQUES TO PERSUADE WITH POWER:

When using any advanced skill or technique, it is imperative you have mastered the fundamental skills that lead to the mastery.

To persuade others, you must believe in yourself. You must believe what you must say is of value and worthy of sharing. You must be self-confident and aware that you will probably receive resistance to your ideas. Not everybody thinks the same way, and what is important to one person may have no value to others. You must be assertive in getting your needs met or communicating your message when others would prevent or discourage you from doing so. You need to have well-developed writing and oral communication skills to persuade others to follow your suggestions.

As in my other publications, I take what I call the 'onion' method of discussing a topic. I start with an overview and then peel away the layers. Each chapter is standalone, and it's unnecessary to read the book lineally. You can use the chapter headings as a reference directory, letting you read specific topics.

I also take an iterative approach, where the content may be viewed from several perspectives.

Onwards and upwards!

Rae A. Stonehouse

Author

April 2023

THE STRUCTURE OF PERSUASION

The structure of persuasion involves three key steps: isolating the problem, identifying the cause, and formulating workable solutions. Let's look closely at each step and provide examples to illustrate the points made by John William Coleman in The Seven Habits of Persuasive Speakers in The Toastmaster, December 2005).

1) Isolate the problem(s) To persuade your audience, first show that a problem exists. To do this effectively, you need to isolate the problem, underline its urgency and severity, and show why it is significant to your audience.

For example, if you are advocating for better mental health support in schools, you might isolate the problem by focusing on the high rates of anxiety and depression among students. You could then underline the urgency and severity of the problem by highlighting the negative impact it has on students' academic performance and overall well-being. Finally, you could show why the problem is significant to your audience by explaining how it affects parents, teachers, and the wider community

. . .

2. **Identify the cause(s)** Once you have established the problem, you need to identify its causes. This requires limiting your causes, logically connecting them to the problem, arguing with sensitivity, and keeping them compelling.

For example, if you are advocating for better mental health support in schools, you might identify the causes by pointing out the lack of resources and training for teachers, the stigma surrounding mental health issues, and the pressure students feel to succeed academically. You would need to logically connect these causes to the problem by showing how they contribute to the high rates of anxiety and depression among students. You would also need to argue with sensitivity, acknowledging that some members of the audience may be connected to the root causes of the problem. Finally, you would need to keep the causes compelling by using rhetorical questions and other persuasive techniques.

3. **Formulate workable solutions** Once you have established the problem and identified its causes, you need to provide your audience with actionable, personable, and immediate solutions.

For example, if you are advocating for better mental health support in schools, you might formulate workable solutions by proposing that schools provide more resources and training for teachers, educate students and parents about mental health issues, and create a supportive and inclusive school culture. You would need to make these solutions actionable by providing specific steps that schools and individuals can take to start them. You would also need to make them personal by showing how they would help students, teachers, and the wider community. Finally, you would need to give them immediacy by emphasizing the importance of acting now rather than later.

Here is a community response based on the above example:

. . .

Improving Mental Health Support in High Schools

Mental health issues affect millions of young people worldwide, and high schools can be challenging environments for students struggling. One organization that recognized this challenge and sought to address it is the Mental Health Association (MHA) in the United States. The MHA's mission is to promote mental health through education, advocacy, research, and service.

To improve mental health support in high schools, the MHA developed a comprehensive program that focuses on providing resources, training, and education for teachers, students, and parents. The program aims to create a supportive and inclusive school culture that focuses on mental health and wellness.

The program offers specific steps that schools and individuals can take to start improving mental health support. For example, schools can incorporate mental health education into their curriculum, offer mental health resources and support groups, and establish policies that focus on mental health and well-being.

Teachers can receive training on identifying and addressing mental health concerns in their students, creating a safe and supportive classroom environment, and accessing resources for their own mental health needs.

Parents can be educated on the signs and symptoms of mental health issues in their children, how to talk to their children about mental health, and how to access mental health resources and support.

By providing actionable solutions that are personalized and immediate, the MHA's program has succeeded in improving mental health support in high schools. Students, teachers, and parents have reported feeling more supported and empowered to address mental health concerns, and schools have reported a decrease in disciplinary incidents and an increase in academic performance.

Advocating for better mental health support in schools is crucial for the well-being of students and the wider community. The MHA's program offers a practical and effective approach that can be replicated in other schools and communities.

∼

2

UNDERSTANDING THE PSYCHOLOGY OF PERSUASION

THE PRINCIPLES OF PERSUASION: UNCOVERING THE SIX PRINCIPLES OF INFLUENCE THAT ARE USED TO PERSUADE AND INFLUENCE OTHERS:

As social beings, we are constantly seeking to persuade and be persuaded in our interactions with others. Be it for personal or professional gain, persuasion plays a significant role in our daily lives. The principles of persuasion, originally introduced by social psychologist Robert Cialdini, are six key tactics that individuals can use to persuade and influence others. These principles are:

1. **Reciprocity** - People feel required to repay others for what they have received. By providing something of value to another person, they are more likely to return the favor.

2. **Authority** - People are more likely to follow the lead of someone who seems credible and knowledgeable in a certain area. Showing knowledge or qualifications in a particular field can increase your authority and likelihood of being influential.

3. **Social Proof** - People are highly influenced by the actions of those around them. If a person sees others engaging in a certain action or behavior, they are more likely to follow.

4. **Consistency** - People have a desire to be consistent in their behaviors and beliefs. By aligning a request or proposal with a person's existing beliefs or earlier actions, they are more likely to comply.

5. **Liking** - People are more likely to be persuaded by those they like and find attractive. Building rapport, finding common ground, and making a personal connection can increase your influence.

6. **Scarcity** - People perceive things as being more valuable if they are rare or hard to obtain. By emphasizing the limited availability of a product or service, people may be more likely to act quickly to obtain it.

By understanding and using these principles of persuasion, individuals can increase their ability to influence others and achieve desired outcomes. However, note that these tactics are most effective when used ethically and with consideration for the needs and desires of the person being persuaded.

THE POWER OF SOCIAL PROOF: HOW THE OPINIONS AND ACTIONS OF OTHERS CAN INFLUENCE OUR OWN DECISIONS AND BEHAVIOR:

Social proof is the phenomenon where people follow the opinions, actions, and behaviors of others to conform to social norms. We can see this in a variety of situations, such as when deciding what to wear, where to eat, or which product to buy.

The power of social proof is immense, as it has been shown to have a significant impact on our decision-making processes. This phenomenon is rooted in our nature as social creatures, as we are more likely to trust and accept the opinions of those around us. For example, if we observe many people queuing up to buy a certain product, we are more likely to perceive it as being good and worth buying even if it does not meet our preferences.

Similarly, social proof can greatly influence our behavior. For example, if we see that everyone around us is following a particular trend, we may be more inclined to do the same. This can lead to the creation and reinforcement of cultural practices, styles, and customs.

In today's world, marketers and businesses are aware of the power of social proof and often use it to their advantage. Testimonials, reviews, and ratings are examples of how social proof is used in marketing to build trust and credibility for products and services.

The power of social proof highlights the importance of social influence and how our behavior can be shaped by the opinions and actions of others. We should remain aware of this phenomenon and try to make sure we are making informed decisions based on our own needs and preferences.

THE ROLE OF EMOTIONS IN PERSUASION: UNDERSTANDING HOW EMOTIONS CAN BE USED TO INFLUENCE OTHERS' PERCEPTIONS & DECISION-MAKING:

Emotions play a significant role in persuasion. They have the power to influence an individual's thinking, perceptions, and decision-making abilities. Using emotions in persuasion is not new and has been around for centuries.

Advertisements, marketing strategies, and political campaigns are all designed to tap into people's emotions to persuade them to act. People are more likely to decide based on their emotions rather than facts or logic. So understanding how emotions can influence others is critical in any form of persuasion.

Leading with emotions lets individuals connect with their audience on a deeper level. It sets the tone for the message and helps to build a relationship between the persuader and the persuaded. Emotions can evoke feelings of happiness, sadness, fear, anger, or excitement, depending on the situation. Skilled persuaders capitalize on these emotions to influence the outcome of the interaction.

For example, an advertisement for a new car may use emotions to create a sense of excitement and adventure. The commercial may depict a family embarking on a road trip, having fun, and enjoying each other's company while driving the new car. In this way, the advertisement appeals to the audience's emotions of happiness and excitement.

But a political campaign may use emotions such as fear or anger to persuade voters. The campaign may use scare tactics to convince the audience that a particular candidate is a threat to their safety, property, or way of life.

Ultimately, using emotions in persuasion can have both positive and negative outcomes. Skilled persuaders understand when and how to use emotions to make their message more effective. If used correctly, emotions can be a powerful tool in persuasion, but they must be used ethically and with consideration for the well-being of others.

COGNITIVE BIASES AND HEURISTICS: RECOGNIZING THE COMMON THOUGHT PROCESSES THAT CAN LEAD PEOPLE TO MAKE DECISIONS BASED ON FLAWED LOGIC OR INCOMPLETE INFORMATION:

Cognitive biases and heuristics are common thought processes that can lead people to decide based on flawed logic or incomplete information. These biases are often automatic and subconscious, so people may not even be aware of them. Understanding these biases and heuristics is crucial for making better decisions and avoiding common pitfalls.

One of the most common cognitive biases is confirmation bias, which is the tendency to seek information that confirms our beliefs and ignore information that doesn't. This bias can lead us to decide based on incomplete or inaccurate information and can also prevent us from considering alternative viewpoints.

Another common cognitive bias is the availability heuristic, which is the tendency to decide based on easily available or recent information.

This bias can lead us to overestimate the likelihood of rare events and underestimate the likelihood of more common events.

Other cognitive biases include anchoring bias, which occurs when we rely too heavily on the first piece of information we receive when making a decision, and framing effect, which occurs when the way information is presented affects our decision-making.

Heuristics are mental shortcuts that let us make decisions quickly and efficiently, but they can also lead to mistakes. For example, the representativeness heuristic is the tendency to make judgments based on how well something conforms to a familiar stereotype or prototype. This heuristic can lead us to overlook important information that doesn't fit our preconceived notions.

Understanding cognitive biases and heuristics is critical for making better decisions. By recognizing these common thought processes, we can avoid errors caused by flawed logic or incomplete information and make more rational decisions.

PERSUASION IN MARKETING: EXPLORING HOW COMPANIES USE TECHNIQUES OF PERSUASION AND INFLUENCE IN ADVERTISING AND SALES TACTICS

Marketing involves persuasive tactics and influence to appeal to consumers and drive sales. Often, companies use various techniques in advertising and sales tactics to persuade consumers to buy their products. Here are techniques that companies use to persuade consumers:

1. Appeal to Emotions: Emotional appeal is a powerful tool that companies use to influence consumers. They use images or words that stimulate positive emotions like happiness, joy, love, or humor to make people feel good about the product. This persuasion can be seen in commercials or print ads.

2. Authority: Companies use people with authority or celebrity status to promote a product or to appear in an advertisement. Using a celebrity to endorse a product or brand can instill trust in the brand by association.

3. Social Proof: Companies often use the social proof technique, which is the idea that people are more likely to do something if others are doing it too. For example, an advertisement might say that "9 out of 10 people recommend our product," which can give consumers the impression that the product is popular.

4. Scarcity: Consumers' sense of urgency can be heightened by highlighting the scarcity of a product. This could involve emphasizing limited edition products or creating an artificial scarcity to create the impression of demand.

5. Reciprocity: Companies use the principle of reciprocity, which is the idea that people are more likely to make a purchase if they feel they have received something in return. For example, offering a free sample of a product can create a sense of duty in the consumer to buy it.

Companies use a range of persuasion techniques in marketing and sales to drive sales and appeal to consumers. Understanding the techniques used can help consumers to remain objective as they decide on what products to buy.

ETHICAL CONSIDERATIONS: DISCUSSING THE POTENTIAL ETHICAL CONCERNS AND RESPONSIBILITIES THAT COME WITH USING PERSUASION TECHNIQUES IN PERSONAL OR PROFESSIONAL CONTEXTS

Using persuasion techniques has become a common practice in personal and professional contexts. We can define persuasion as the act of influencing someone's beliefs, attitudes, or behaviors through a variety of techniques or strategies. However, like any other approach, ethical considerations must be considered when using persuasion techniques.

One of the primary ethical concerns is transparency. Persuasion strategies can vary in their level of transparency; some techniques can be subtle and even deceptive, while others may be more open and transparent. In professional contexts, it is essential to be transparent about persuasive techniques on colleagues or clients, as secrecy can lead to unethical behavior and miscommunication.

Another ethical consideration is autonomy. Persuasion can affect people's decisions, and it is essential to make sure individuals have the freedom to make their own choices. Coercing or manipulating individuals to adopt a particular perspective is not ethical and can lead to long-term negative consequences.

Another ethical consideration is respect. When using persuasion techniques, it is crucial to maintain respect for individuals and their beliefs. Disrespecting views and beliefs and trying to convert individuals to a different perspective can lead to ethical issues.

Finally, ethical use of persuasion techniques includes honesty, fairness and the duty to act in good faith. Persuasion must be used with an understanding of the consequences and responsibilities that come with it.

Persuasion techniques can be an effective tool when used ethically and responsibly. The foundation of ethical persuasion is transparency, respect, autonomy, honesty, and fairness. By following these principles, individuals can use persuasion techniques to meet their goals while maintaining ethical standards.

APPLYING THE PRINCIPLES OF PERSUASION: OFFERING PRACTICAL TIPS AND STRATEGIES FOR USING THESE PRINCIPLES ETHICALLY AND EFFECTIVELY IN OUR OWN LIVES AND WORK:

Persuasion is an essential skill in any personal or business interaction, and its effectiveness can be maximized by applying specific principles to our approach. While the outcome of persuasive attempts can vary depending on the audience, the message, and the context, using persuasion principles can lead to a higher likelihood of success.

Below, we have outlined some of the essential principles of persuasion and offered practical tips and strategies for using them ethically and effectively in our own lives and work.

1. Reciprocity:

Reciprocity is a basic human instinct that involves the need to repay what has been given to us. When someone does something nice for us, we feel a sense of duty to do something in return. To use the principle of reciprocity effectively in persuasion, offer something of value to your audience before asking for something in return. This could be as simple as providing a compliment or a thoughtful gesture. By starting the exchange of goodwill, you are likely to get a positive response from your audience.

2. Scarcity:

Scarcity is the principle that people tend to place more value on things limited or rare. To use this principle effectively in persuasion, emphasize the unique features and benefits of what you are offering and highlight the exclusivity of the opportunity. However, it is crucial to make sure the scarcity is genuinely limited, or rare, as false claims can harm your credibility and ultimately backfire.

3. Authority:

Authority is the principle of persuasion that involves citing trustworthy sources or experts to convince your audience of your points. To use this principle effectively in persuasion, position yourself or your brand as a reliable source and be ready to provide evidence or examples to support your claims. Be transparent in your knowledge or qualifications and avoid making false or exaggerated assertions, as it can damage your credibility.

4. Consistency:

Consistency is the principle of persuasion that involves aligning your message with the values and beliefs of your audience. To use this principle effectively, highlight the shared values or interests between you and your audience and show how your message aligns with these.

Emphasize the importance of maintaining consistency in your message and actions and avoid contradicting yourself, which can lead to confusion and distrust.

5. Social Proof:

Social proof is the principle that people follow the actions of others, especially those who are like themselves. To use social proof effectively in persuasion, highlight the positive experiences of others who have used your product or service and leverage their testimonials to show the effectiveness of your solutions. Be careful not to manipulate the evidence or fabricate testimonials, as it can be easily detected and diminish your credibility.

Understanding and applying the principles of persuasion can significantly enhance our ability to influence and persuade others. However, we must strive to apply these principles ethically and responsibly, respecting the individual autonomy and decision-making capacity of our audience. By using these principles effectively and consistently, we can build trust, credibility, and meaningful relationships with our audience.

3

CRAFTING A COMPELLING SPEECH OUTLINE

UNDERSTANDING THE PURPOSE & CONTEXT OF YOUR SPEECH:

As a speaker, it is important to understand the purpose and context of your speech. Your purpose is the goal you intend to achieve through your presentation, while the context is the situation or setting in which the speech is delivered. Understanding these two elements can help you tailor your message to your audience and make sure you achieve your desired results.

Your purpose should be clear and specific. Are you trying to inform, persuade, entertain, or inspire your audience? Knowing your purpose will help you determine what content to include in your speech and how to present it. If you are trying to inform your audience, for example, you will want to focus on providing facts, data, and examples that support your message. If you are trying to persuade them, you will need to understand their values, beliefs, and attitudes and craft a message that resonates with them.

Once you have identified your purpose, you can then consider the context of your speech. What is the occasion or event? Who is your audience? What is their level of knowledge or interest in the topic? Understanding these factors will help you adapt your message to your audience and make it relevant to their needs and interests. If you are speaking at a conference, for example, you may need to use technical language and provide detailed information. If you are speaking to a general audience, you may need to use simpler language and provide more context to make sure everyone can understand your message.

Understanding the purpose and context of your speech is essential for delivering a successful presentation. It will help you tailor your message to your audience, make sure your message resonates with them, and achieve your desired results. Take the time to identify your purpose and consider your audience and the setting in which you will speak, and you will be well on your way to delivering a powerful and effective speech.

BRAINSTORMING & STRUCTURING YOUR IDEAS:

1. Start with a topic or problem you want to address. Write down everything you already know about the subject, and then think of questions you still have. This will help you frame your thinking around the topic.

2. Use mind mapping techniques to generate new ideas. Start with a central idea and then branch out to related topics or subtopics. This can be done manually using pen and paper or digitally using mind mapping tools like MindMeister or Coggle.

3. Brainstorm with a group. Get with peers or colleagues who can help you generate new ideas. Encourage everyone to contribute freely, without worrying about judgment or criticism.

4. Use SWOT analysis, which stands for Strengths, Weaknesses, Opportunities, and Threats. List everything that applies to your topic in these categories. This will help you identify potential obstacles and opportunities as you move forward.

5. Use a structured approach to organizing your ideas. This could involve creating an outline, flowchart, or spreadsheet. This will help

you see how each idea connects to the next and determine the best order to present your ideas to your audience.

6. Seek feedback on your ideas from trusted sources. Share your ideas with peers or mentors who can provide constructive criticism and help you refine your thinking. This could be done in a one-on-one session, a workshop, or a group coaching setting.

By incorporating these tips into your brainstorming and structuring process, you will find that coming up with innovative ideas becomes easier.

IDENTIFYING KEY POINTS AND SUPPORTING EVIDENCE:

Identifying key points and supporting evidence is a vital skill when analyzing or summarizing a piece of literature or research paper. To identify key points, you need to understand the main argument or message in the text, and then break it down into its essential parts. Supporting evidence is the data, statistics, and facts that back up the key points.

1. Read the text carefully: Before you can identify the key points and supporting evidence, you need to have a deep understanding of the text. Read the text carefully, paying attention to the main argument or message.

2. Identify the main argument or message: Once you have read the text, try to identify the main argument or message. This is usually the central idea that the author is trying to communicate.

3. Break the argument or message down into its essential parts: Once you have identified the main argument or message, try to break it down into its essential parts. These are the key points that support the main argument.

4. Look for supporting evidence: For each key point, look for supporting evidence. This may include data, statistics, facts, or quotes from other sources that back up the point being made.

5. Evaluate the supporting evidence: Once you have identified the supporting evidence, evaluate it to make sure it is credible and reliable. This will help you determine the overall quality of the argument being presented.

By identifying key points and supporting evidence, you can gain a deeper understanding of a text and better evaluate the quality of the argument being presented. This skill is essential for critical reading and analysis and can be applied to a wide range of texts, from literature to scientific research papers.

CREATING AN ENGAGING INTRODUCTION & MEMORABLE CONCLUSION:

Creating an engaging introduction and a memorable conclusion is crucial to any piece of writing. Not only does it grab the reader's attention, but it also leaves a lasting impression. Here are tips on how to craft an introduction and conclusion that will keep readers interested:

1. Start with a hook: The first sentence of your introduction should be attention-grabbing. Consider using a shocking statistic, quote, or anecdote to draw in the reader.

2. Provide context: Once you have their attention, provide background information that sets the stage for your topic. Define any key terms or ideas that readers might not be familiar with.

3. Make a thesis statement: Your thesis statement should be clear, concise, and arguable. It should state your main argument or point and what you hope to achieve through your writing.

4. Sum up your main points: In your conclusion, summarize your main points and restate your thesis in a fresh way. This reminds the reader of what you've said while emphasizing the importance of your message.

5. End with a bang: Your final sentence should be memorable and thought-provoking. Consider using a call to action, a rhetorical question, or a powerful quote that leaves a lasting impression.

Overall, by crafting an engaging introduction and a memorable conclusion, you can create a piece of writing that leaves a lasting impact on your readers.

USING TRANSITIONS TO CONNECT IDEAS & MAINTAIN FLOW:

Transitions play a crucial role in making your writing clear, concise, and coherent. These elements help to connect your ideas, thoughts, and arguments while maintaining the flow and logical progression of your writing. Here are essential tips on how to use transitions effectively:

First, start by understanding the type of transition best suited to connect your ideas. For example, you can use a contrast transition when introducing opposing arguments. Similarly, you can use a chronological transition when presenting a timeline of events.

Second, use simple and straightforward transitions to help your readers understand your flow quickly. Words such as "however", "meanwhile," and "thus" are good examples of sentence connectors that can denote different relationships between ideas.

Third, avoid using too many transitions. While transitions can significantly improve your writing, including too many, can make your work seem robotic, and can even distract your readers from the main message of your writing.

Last, always take the time to review and revise your work to make sure your transitions create a cohesive flow throughout your writing. Proofreading your work can help you spot any obvious errors and typos and make your writing much more readable and pleasing to your readers.

Using transitions can make a significant difference to the clarity, conciseness, and coherence of your writing. By following these tips, you can create a more structured and logical writing style that engages and informs your readers.

INCORPORATING VISUAL AIDS & EXAMPLES:

Incorporating visual aids and examples can significantly enhance a presentation or written material as it provides readers or listeners with a better understanding of the topic. Visual aids such as graphs, diagrams, and pictures give a clear picture of the data, making it more accessible to those with learning disabilities.

Similarly, using relevant examples can illustrate the point being made, making it easier for the audience to relate to the topic. For example, while discussing an idea or a theory, providing examples that the audience can understand will show how the theory applies in the real world.

The critical part of incorporating visual aids and examples is to make sure they are relevant and easy to comprehend. Using complex graphics or examples that are too specific can cause confusion and even boredom. Thus, simplicity is vital when using visual aids and examples.

Visual aids and examples can also aid in stimulating the audience's interest and engagement and help them to remember the topic long after the presentation has ended. They can provide a welcome break from reading or listening to a slew of plain texts.

Incorporating visual aids and examples is an effective method to enhance your presentation or written material. They can provide an added dimension to your work and help you to communicate your message effectively.

REVISING AND POLISHING YOUR SPEECH OUTLINE TO ENSURE CLARITY & IMPACT:

Incorporating visual aids and examples can significantly enhance a presentation or written material as it provides readers or listeners with a better understanding of the topic. Visual aids such as graphs, diagrams, and pictures give a clear picture of the data, making it more accessible to those with learning disabilities.

Similarly, using relevant examples can illustrate the point being made, making it easier for the audience to relate to the topic. For example, while discussing an idea or a theory, providing examples that the audience can understand will show how the theory applies in the real world.

The critical part of incorporating visual aids and examples is to make sure they are relevant and easy to comprehend. Using complex graphics or examples too specific can cause confusion and even boredom. Thus, simplicity is vital when using visual aids and examples.

Visual aids and examples can also aid in stimulating the audience's interest and engagement and help them to remember the topic long after the presentation has ended. They can provide a welcome break from reading or listening to a slew of plain texts.

Incorporating visual aids and examples is an effective method to enhance your presentation or written material. They can provide an added dimension to your work and help you to communicate your message effectively.

～

❧ 4 ❧
USING RHETORICAL DEVICES TO ENHANCE PERSUASION

INTRODUCTION TO PERSUASIVE WRITING AND WHY RHETORICAL DEVICES ARE CRUCIAL:

As a writer, you must often persuade an audience to believe in your arguments or act based on your words. Persuasive writing is a crucial skill to have in both personal and professional contexts, and it requires an understanding of the art of rhetoric. By using rhetorical devices, writers can effectively convey their messages and sway the opinions of their readers or listeners. These devices can evoke an emotional response, inspire empathy or admiration, and provide logical reasons for taking a particular course of action. In this context, knowing how to use and apply rhetorical devices is essential for effective persuasive writing. So, as a writer, it is crucial to learn and understand the different rhetorical devices to make your writing more compelling and influential.

UNDERSTANDING THE MOST POPULAR RHETORICAL DEVICES: ETHOS, PATHOS, & LOGOS

Rhetorical devices are techniques that a speaker or writer uses to enhance their arguments and make them more persuasive to their audience. Ethos, pathos, and logos are three of the most popular and effective rhetorical devices used in communication.

Ethos refers to the credibility or trustworthiness of the speaker or writer. The audience is more likely to believe and accept the arguments presented if they perceive the speaker/writer as honest, knowledgeable, and reliable. Ethos is established by showing knowledge, authority, or experience in a particular subject matter. Using supporting evidence, citing reliable sources, or drawing from personal experience are ways to establish ethos.

Pathos involves appealing to the audience's emotions. Pathos tries to create an emotional reaction in the audience that connects them with the speaker/writer's arguments. A speaker/writer can use vivid language, personal anecdotes, or powerful imagery to evoke emotions such as joy, fear, anger, or compassion. Pathos is particularly effective in speeches, advertisements, or any situation that requires the audience to act.

Logos refers to logical and rational arguments supported by facts, data, or evidence. Logos tries to persuade the audience using reasoning and evidence. A speaker/writer can use analogies, statistics, or deductive reasoning to make a logical case. Logos is effective when trying to convince an audience of a particular viewpoint. Logos is often used in academic writing, debates, or persuasive essays.

Ethos, pathos, and logos are essential rhetorical devices that speakers and writers use to persuade their audience. They are powerful tools that can influence perceptions, evoke emotions and make logical arguments. Effective communication often involves all three of these techniques in a balanced way to achieve the desired effect on the audience.

HOW TO USE ETHOS TO ESTABLISH CREDIBILITY AND PERSUADE THROUGH CHARACTER & AUTHORITY:

Ethos is an effective persuasive tool that relies on building credibility and trust with your audience. Ethos refers to your character or authority that makes people believe in your views and accept your opinions. Here are ways to use ethos to establish credibility and persuade your audience:

1. Establish knowledge: Demonstrate knowledge and expertise in your field by providing evidence, statistics, or research to support your argument. This helps to build credibility and trust with your audience.

2. Use reputable sources: Use trustworthy and reliable sources to support your argument. Cite sources from credible and respected organizations, experts, or scholars in your field.

3. Highlight shared values: Appeal to your audience's shared values and beliefs. Address their concerns and show how your views align with their beliefs, interests, or goals.

4. Personal experience: Share personal stories or experiences to support your argument. This helps to create a personal connection and establish credibility with your audience, making them more likely to relate to your views.

5. Be confident and passionate: Show confidence and passion when presenting your argument. This helps to create a positive impression and establishes you as a credible and authoritative figure in your field.

Using ethos to establish credibility and persuade through character and authority, you can connect with your audience on a personal level and convince them to accept and support your views.

THE ROLE OF PATHOS IN EVOKING EMOTIONS AND CREATING A CONNECTION WITH THE AUDIENCE:

Pathos is a powerful tool that speakers use to evoke strong emotions in their audience. It is an appeal to the emotions of people, and it is one of the fundamental elements of persuasive communication. Pathos is a powerful way to connect with an audience because it makes people feel understood and confirmed. When people are emotionally invested in a message, they are more likely to remember and believe what is being said.

One reason pathos is so effective is that emotions are universal. Everyone has emotions, and everyone can relate to experiencing strong feelings. By appealing to the emotional experiences of an audience, speakers can create an immediate connection that transcends any differences that may exist between them.

Pathos works by tapping into a range of different emotions. Some common emotions that speakers may target include sadness, anger, fear, and happiness. Depending on the goals of a speech, different emotions may be more effective at achieving the desired outcome. For example, a speaker trying to persuade people to support a social cause may use pathos to evoke feelings of empathy and compassion for those suffering.

Another way that pathos can create a connection with an audience is by personalizing a message. By sharing personal stories or experiences that tap into shared emotions, speakers can make their message more relatable and poignant. When speakers share their personal struggles and challenges, it humanizes them and makes them more approachable.

Ultimately, the role of pathos in evoking emotions and creating a connection with an audience is to move people to action. By inspiring strong emotions and connecting with people on a personal level, speakers can motivate their audience to act, whether it is to support a cause, change their own lives, or to help others.

HOW TO APPLY LOGOS TO STRUCTURE COMPELLING ARGUMENTS AND PERSUADE THROUGH FACTS & REASON:

As a writer or speaker, your ability to apply logos is crucial to your ability to persuade your audience. Here's how you can structure compelling arguments and persuade through facts and reason:

1. Start with a clear thesis statement. Your argument should be clearly stated in the opening statement of your speech or essay.

2. Use logical reasoning. Logos is built on logical reasoning, and your argument should be logically sound. Your evidence should be relevant, sufficient and accurate to support your claim.

3. Use empirical evidence. Use facts, statistics, and other empirical evidence to support your point. Cite your sources and make it clear that you have done your research.

4. Use analogies and comparisons. Using analogies and comparisons can be an effective way to help your audience understand complex ideas.

5. Address counterarguments. Acknowledge the potential objections or counterarguments to your argument and address them directly. This will show you have taken opposing views seriously and that you are confident in your own argument.

6. Use clear, concise language. Make your point clearly and simply. Avoid technical jargon, convoluted sentences or any other barriers to clear communication.

7. Use visual aids. Graphics, charts or other visual aids can make complex or abstract ideas more tangible, increasing the persuasiveness of your argument.

8. End with a powerful conclusion that summarizes your argument and reinforces your position. A strong conclusion can leave a lasting impression on your audience.

By following these steps, you can apply logos in your arguments and persuade your audience through facts and reason.

THE USE OF RHETORICAL QUESTIONS, IRONY, AND REPETITION TO ADD TO THE PERSUASIVE IMPACT OF A SPEECH OR TEXT:

Rhetorical questions, irony, and repetition are powerful rhetorical devices that can enhance the persuasive impact of a speech or text. These devices are used to capture the attention of the audience, create an emotional response, and encourage them to act.

Rhetorical questions are questions that do not require an answer, but instead are used to provoke thought and encourage the audience to think critically about a particular topic. They can effectively engage the audience and lead them to the desired conclusion. For example, in a speech about climate change, a speaker may ask, "Do we really want to leave our children and grandchildren a planet that is in worse shape than the one we inherited?"

Irony is a powerful tool that can create a contrast between what is expected and what actually happens. Irony is especially effective when used to expose hypocrisy or to point out the absurdity of a situation. For example, a politician who champions family values, but is caught in a scandal involving infidelity, can be exposed using irony.

Repetition is the repeated use of words, phrases, or sentences to emphasize a point or idea. Repetition can create a sense of rhythm and intensity that can be persuasive. For example, a speech about the importance of education can use the repetition of the phrase "education is the key to success" to emphasize the point.

Overall, using rhetorical questions, irony, and repetition can significantly enhance the persuasive impact of a speech or text. These devices can engage the audience, create an emotional response, and encourage them to act. When used effectively, they can make a speech or text more memorable and persuasive.

CASE STUDIES OF FAMOUS SPEECHES AND HOW THEY EFFECTIVELY APPLIED RHETORICAL DEVICES FOR PERSUASION:

Public speaking has been a crucial element of human communication since the evolution of the language itself. Millions of speeches have been delivered on various occasions, but only a few were powerful enough to shape the world's history. The reason behind the success of these speeches is not merely their content but also the use of persuasive techniques or rhetorical devices. Rhetorical devices are tools that speakers employ to communicate their message in a compelling and persuasive way. In this article, we will explore three famous speeches of history that employed these strategies effectively.

1. "I have a dream" by Martin Luther King Jr.

Dr. Martin Luther King Jr.'s "I have a dream" speech is one of the most iconic and powerful speeches in the history of public speaking. King delivered this speech on August 28, 1963, during the March on Washington for Jobs and Freedom. The aim of this speech was to motivate people to fight for racial equality and justice. King's message was a call to action and was delivered very persuasively. The speech was packed with rhetorical devices, including:

Repetition: King repeated the phrase "I have a dream" several times throughout the speech, emphasizing his vision of a world where people of all races lived together in harmony.

Metaphors: King used several metaphors throughout his speech. For example, he compared racial inequality to a bad check that America had given to its citizens and used the idea of a "slumbering freedom" that needed to be awakened.

Antithesis: King used antithesis to create a contrast between the present situation and his dream of a better world. For example, he said, "We must not be guilty of injustice or violence but let us love one another."

2. "The Gettysburg Address" by Abraham Lincoln

Abraham Lincoln's "The Gettysburg Address" ranks as one of the most memorable speeches in American history. It was delivered on November 19, 1863, in the aftermath of the battle of Gettysburg. The aim of the speech was to honor the soldiers who had lost their lives in the battle and to reinforce the union's cause to end slavery. The speech is short, but its impact was enormous, and it had several rhetorical devices, including:

Anaphora: Lincoln repeated the phrase "we cannot dedicate, we cannot consecrate, we cannot hallow" to emphasize the sacrifices made by the soldiers who fought in Gettysburg.

Parallelism: Lincoln used parallelism to compare the present situation to the past and believed that "this nation, under God, shall have a new birth of freedom, and that government of the people, by the people, for the people, shall not perish from the earth."

3. "Blood, Toil, Tears, and Sweat" by Winston Churchill

Winston Churchill's "Blood, Toil, Tears, and Sweat" speech was delivered in the House of Commons on May 13, 1940. Churchill had just become the British Prime Minister and was addressing the members of parliament to prepare them for the upcoming war against Germany. The aim of the speech was to motivate and inspire the British people to fight bravely and never surrender. Churchill employed several rhetorical devices, including:

Imagery: Churchill used strong and vivid images to describe the upcoming war. For example, he said, "I have nothing to offer but blood, toil, tears, and sweat."

Rhetorical questions: Churchill used rhetorical questions to challenge his audience and inspire them. For example, he said, "You ask, what is our aim? I can answer in one word: victory."

Conclusion:

. . .

The three speeches mentioned above provide shining examples of what can be achieved through effective rhetorical devices. These famous speeches still hold their power and persuade people today, years after they were first delivered. Their use of rhetorical devices illustrates that the art of public speaking is not just about inform, but also affect and influence.

5

THE POWER OF STORYTELLING IN PERSUASIVE SPEAKING

THE IMPORTANCE OF STORYTELLING IN RELATABILITY:

Storytelling can help to make a speech more relatable to an audience by creating emotional connections between the idea presented and lived experiences. This process can help to humanize your message and make it more memorable.

As humans, we are wired to love stories. From our earliest childhood years, we are captivated by narratives that transport us away from our own lives, letting us see the world through the eyes of another.

And for this reason, storytelling is so important in relatability. Whether it's a work of fiction or a personal anecdote, stories let us connect on a deeper level with those around us. They explain the experiences and emotions of others, helping us to empathize and understand their perspectives.

In today's fast-paced world, where social media and digital communication dominate our interactions, storytelling has become more important than ever. It lets us step back from the noise and distractions of everyday life and connect with others profoundly.

Whether it's sharing our own story or listening to someone else's, storytelling creates a space for genuine human connection. It lets us see each other as complex and nuanced individuals, with our own struggles, triumphs, and unique perspectives on the world.

In a world that can often feel fragmented and disconnected, storytelling has the power to bring us together. It reminds us of our shared humanity and the importance of empathy and understanding in our interactions with others.

So, whether you're sharing your own experiences or listening to someone else's, never underestimate the power of storytelling in forging meaningful connections and creating a more relatable and compassionate world.

THE ROLE OF STORYTELLING IN ENGAGEMENT:

Storytelling can help to hold an audience's attention by creating a powerful narrative that draws them into the speaker's world. This process can be useful in keeping an audience engaged and invested in the speech at hand.

Storytelling is a powerful tool for engaging audiences, whether at work or in everyday life. Stories help us to interpret and make sense of information, and they let us connect with others on an emotional level. The role of storytelling in engagement is multifaceted and can be seen in many contexts.

One of the keyways storytelling can drive engagement is by helping to identify the needs of the audience. When a story is crafted to appeal to a specific group of people, it can resonate with them in a way that traditional communication methods cannot. For example, if you're trying to engage a group of employees, you might use a story that relates to their interests, challenges, or experiences. This could include personal anecdotes, real world examples, or even historical stories.

Storytelling can also help to build trust between the storyteller and the audience. By sharing personal stories or experiences, you can show your empathy and understanding of the audience's perspective. This can go a long way in building rapport and creating a sense of community.

A well-told story can also have a powerful impact on the emotions of the audience. Stories that tap into universal fears or desires will evoke a wide variety of emotions, from joy and excitement to sadness and fear. This emotional connection can be leveraged to motivate people to act or change their lives.

Finally, storytelling can be a highly effective tool for education and training. When information is presented as a story, it is easier to remember and keep. This is because stories provide a context and a narrative structure that helps to anchor information in the brain.

Storytelling plays a vital role in engagement. By using stories to connect with our audiences, we can foster trust, build community, and motivate people to act. Whether we are trying to educate, entertain, or persuade, storytelling is a powerful tool that should not be overlooked.

THE IMPACT OF STORYTELLING ON THE OVERALL MESSAGE:

Storytelling can help to reinforce your message by creating a vivid and memorable image in the mind of the listener. This process can help to tie together the different elements of a persuasive speech and leave a lasting impact on the audience.

Storytelling is an age-old practice that has been integral to human communication for centuries. Stories can inspire, entertain, educate, and provide insight into our cultural background. In today's world, the impact of storytelling on the overall message has become more important than ever before.

At its core, storytelling is a powerful tool for conveying complex messages in a way that engages and resonates with the audience. Stories help to humanize concepts and ideas, making them more relatable and understandable. When done well, storytelling can create a powerful emotional connection that can influence people's beliefs, behaviors, and attitudes.

One of the most significant impacts of storytelling on the overall message is that it can help organizations to communicate their values and mission more effectively. By weaving stories that align with their core principles, businesses and organizations can create a narrative that presents a compelling reason for their existence. A powerful example of this is the mission statement of TOMS shoes, which is to "improve lives by providing basic necessities to those in need." This mission statement is strongly supported by a powerful narrative about the company's founding, which is a core part of TOMS' brand identity.

Another important impact of storytelling on the overall message is that it can help people to empathize with others. By telling stories that explore different cultures, experiences, and perspectives, we can create a shared understanding of the world that can foster greater understanding and empathy. This is particularly important in an era where people are increasingly divided by politics, race, gender, and other factors.

Finally, storytelling can directly affect behavior. By telling stories that encourage action, organizations can inspire people to take positive steps toward a shared goal. For example, charity organizations often use storytelling to encourage people to donate, volunteer, or advocate for specific causes.

The impact of storytelling on the overall message cannot be overstated. By creating narratives that engage, inspire, and educate people, we can create a shared understanding of the world that can drive positive change and social progress. Whether we are telling stories in the boardroom, the classroom, or the community, we all have the power to make a difference through the power of storytelling.

THE POWER OF VISUAL STORYTELLING:

Visual storytelling can help to create a vivid picture of your message for your audience. This process can be useful in highlighting key points or ideas that might be difficult to convey in words alone.

Visual storytelling is an art form with the ability to capture the attention and emotions of viewers in a way that words alone often cannot. Through imagery, music, and narration, visual storytelling can create a powerful connection between the storyteller and their audience.

One of the most significant advantages of visual storytelling is that it can convey complex ideas and emotions quickly and effectively. As humans, we are wired to process visual information more easily than other types of information, making images and videos an ideal medium for storytelling.

Visual storytelling can transcend cultural and linguistic barriers. A compelling image or video can communicate a universal message that resonates with people from all walks of life. This is why visual storytelling has become an essential tool for marketers, journalists, and nonprofit organizations to engage and inspire their audiences.

The power of visual storytelling lies not only in its ability to entertain and inform but also in its capacity to effect real change. Through documentaries, for example, visual storytellers have brought attention to various social, economic, and political issues, catalyzing political action and societal reform.

Visual storytelling is a powerful tool with the potential to engage, inform, and inspire people around the world. Whether through online videos, photography, or films, visual storytellers have the power to move people emotionally and drive change.

THE POTENTIAL PITFALLS OF STORYTELLING:

Storytelling can be a powerful tool in the right hands, but it can also manipulate or mislead an audience. It is important for speakers to use storytelling ethically and with integrity.

Storytelling is an ancient tradition used to convey information and entertain audiences for generations. However, like any other form of communication, there are potential pitfalls that storytellers need to be aware of. Here are some of the most common dangers of storytelling:

1. Generalization: Stories can be powerful tools for highlighting important issues, but if they are not carefully constructed, they can perpetuate stereotypes and generalize entire groups of people. A story-teller must be mindful of the danger of portraying any group using shallow, stereotypical characters or tropes.

2. Distortion of facts: Storytelling involves weaving together facts and fiction to create a compelling narrative, but if a storyteller becomes too focused on entertaining the audience, they may distort factual information. This can lead to misunderstanding, confusion or even manipulation of the truth.

3. Oversimplification: Something that may be simple to the story-teller may not always be the same for the audience. A storyteller must be careful not to oversimplify complex issues that can be difficult for audiences to understand. Oversimplification can lead to misunderstanding and misinterpretation, which could ultimately derail the plot.

4. Ignoring the variety of perspectives: Stories shouldn't only uplift or confirm the perspective of one particular group or individual. A storyteller must acknowledge the diversity of life and experiences of all their characters.

5. Perpetuating myths or stereotypes: Storytelling should help bring down barriers and shed light on issues. Yet, one that unnecessarily reinforces stereotypes, whether positive or negative, can do more harm than good.

Stories are powerful, and using them correctly can help advance understanding, empathy, and learning. However, to tell effective stories, one must be concerned about the potential pitfalls that can arise if one is not careful in nuancing the narrative.

THE IMPORTANCE OF AUTHENTICITY IN STORYTELLING:

Storytelling is most effective when it comes from a place of authenticity and personal experience. Speakers who are genuine and honest about their experiences are more likely to connect with their audience and create a lasting impact.

Authenticity is an essential factor in storytelling. It refers to the originality, genuineness, and truthfulness of a narrative. Authentic stories are those that reflect the reality of the human experience and have the power to resonate with the readers. Authenticity in storytelling is essential because it brings credibility to the narrative and helps the reader connect with the characters and their situations.

Authenticity helps to build trust between the storyteller and the audience. In a fictional story, the reader must believe that the characters and events are plausible, and the only way to achieve this is through authenticity. An authentic story enables the reader to relate to the characters' circumstances and understand their motivations, which enhances the reader's emotional connection to the story.

Authentic storytelling helps to break stereotypes and create empathy for characters that the reader may not have related to otherwise. It also provides a platform for marginalized voices to be heard, offering a broader view of the human experience.

Authentic storytelling is not just limited to fiction. It is equally important in non-fiction storytelling such as memoirs, biographies, and historical accounts. In a non-fiction account, the reader must believe that the events and people described are real, and authenticity is paramount in achieving this.

The importance of authenticity in storytelling cannot be overstated. It creates a bond between the storyteller and the reader, evokes emotions, and brings credibility to the narrative. An authentic story provides an opportunity for readers to learn from different perspectives, breaking stereotypes and broadening their understanding of the human experience.

TIPS FOR USING STORYTELLING EFFECTIVELY:

There are several tips and strategies that speakers can use to make their storytelling more effective, including using vivid language, incorporating unexpected twists or turns, and tailoring their stories to the specific needs and interests of their audience.

Know your audience and tailor your story.

As a storyteller, keep in mind the needs and preferences of your audience. Knowing your audience can help you tailor your story, making it more interesting and engaging for them. Use vivid and descriptive language to create mental images for your listeners, as this can make the story more immersive and memorable. Incorporate conflict and tension into your story to keep your audience engaged and curious about what will happen next.

To build trust and connection with your listeners, be authentic and share personal experiences they can relate to. Use humor to lighten the mood and add interest, but make sure it is appropriate to the tone and subject of the story. Use pacing and timing to build suspense and highlight important parts of the story and use repetition and callbacks to reinforce key themes or messages.

Sensory details can make your story more immersive and engaging, so use them to bring your story to life. Practice and rehearse your story to refine your delivery and improve your performance. Finally, use your own unique style and voice to make your story memorable and impactful, and to connect with your audience in a meaningful way.

Use vivid and descriptive language to create mental images for your listeners.

As you speak, think about the words you are using and how they can create a picture in your listener's mind. Use descriptive language that appeals to the senses − sight, sound, taste, smell, and touch − to help your listeners feel as if they are right there with you.

For example, instead of saying "it was a beautiful day," describe the scene in detail: "The sun was shining brightly, casting a warm golden glow over the lush green fields. The air was filled with the sweet scent of wildflowers, and the sound of birds chirping in the trees overhead made it feel like we were in a magical forest."

Or, instead of saying "the food was good," use sensory language to bring the taste to life: "The juicy steak melted in my mouth, packed full of bold flavors that danced on my tongue. The crispy fries were piping hot, with the perfect amount of salt that made them irresistible."

By using vivid and descriptive language, you can create mental images for your listeners that will make your speeches more engaging, memorable, and impactful.

Incorporate conflict and tension to keep your audience engaged.

As a writer, your ultimate goal is to keep your audience engaged and hooked until the very end. One effective way to do this is by incorporating conflict and tension into your writing.

Conflict is the backbone of any good story. It is the driving force that creates tension and creates a sense of urgency to discover what happens next. Conflict can come in different forms, whether it's between characters, within a character's psyche, or external obstacles that hinder the character's goals.

Tension, on the other hand, is the feeling of uncertainty and unease that keeps your readers on edge. It can be created through unresolved conflict, anticipation of a potential threat, or a ticking clock that adds urgency to the story.

By incorporating conflict and tension into your writing, you not only keep your readers engaged but also create a more dynamic and intriguing story. Make sure that your conflicts and tension are consistent throughout the story and are resolved satisfactorily by the end.

Remember, conflict and tension are essential elements of storytelling. Use them wisely, and your readers cannot put your book down.

Be authentic and share personal experiences to build trust and connection with your listeners.

As a speaker or presenter, your goal is to connect with your audience, build trust and credibility. One of the best ways to achieve this is to be authentic and share personal experiences.

Sharing your personal experiences makes you relatable, approachable, and trustworthy. Your listeners feel like they know you on a deeper level and are more likely to trust and connect with you. It also makes your presentation more engaging and memorable.

When sharing personal experiences, choose stories and examples relevant to your topic and show your point. Be honest and transparent about your experiences, both successes, and failures. This can help your audience relate to you on a human level and make your presentation more powerful.

Remember that being authentic doesn't mean you must share everything about your life. Choose stories and experiences appropriate for the context of the presentation and align with your goals.

Being authentic and sharing personal experiences can help you build trust and connection with your listeners. It can also make your presentation more engaging and memorable. So, be yourself and share your stories!

Use humor to lighten the mood and add interest.

Why was the math book sad? Because it had too many problems.

See? Adding a little humor can instantly brighten up a conversation, presentation or even a written piece. It can also make you more relatable to your audience and help capture their attention. Keep it appropriate and not offend anyone.

Use pacing and timing to build suspense and highlight important parts of the story.

As the sun began to set, John knew he had to act quickly. He scanned the dark alley for any signs of danger and quickened his pace. The sound of his footsteps echoed eerily against the brick walls, increasing his tension.

Suddenly, he heard a rustling sound behind him. He turned to see a shadowy figure lurking out of sight. His heart raced as he felt a knot form in the pit of his stomach. Was he being followed?

He tried to keep calm and picked up his pace, hoping to lose his pursuer in the maze of alleys ahead. Every sound seemed ominous, and every shadow felt like a threat. His mind raced, imagining all sorts of terrifying scenarios.

Finally, he reached a well-lit street, filled with people and activity. He breathed a sigh of relief and slowed down, grateful to have escaped whatever danger had been lurking in the shadows.

This scene illustrates how pacing and timing can build suspense and highlight important parts of a story. By slowing down the action and using descriptions to create tension, the writer can increase the reader's sense of anticipation and create a sense of urgency. Similarly, by speeding up the action and using shorter, more direct sentences, the writer can emphasize key turning points in the story and heighten the drama. The result is a more engaging and immersive reading experience that keeps the reader on the edge of their seat until the very end.

Use repetition and callbacks to reinforce key themes or messages.

Repetitions and callbacks are powerful tools that can create a lasting impact on your audience, reinforcing your key themes and messages. By repeating certain phrases or callbacks, you can create a sense of continuity and consistency that can help your message resonate with your audience. Here are tips for using repetition and callbacks effectively:

1. Choose your key phrases carefully: Before you repeat and call back phrases, make sure they are the right ones. Choose key phrases that encapsulate your message and are easy to remember.

2. Use repetition sparingly: Repeating a phrase too often can feel forced and reduce its impact. Use repetition judiciously to emphasize key points.

3. Vary your delivery: While repetition is effective, it can also be tedious. To keep your audience engaged, use variation in your delivery. Change your tone, volume, or inflection to keep your message fresh.

4. Use callbacks to connect ideas: Callbacks are a powerful way to connect ideas and reinforce key themes. By recalling a phrase from earlier in your presentation, you can create links and associations in your audience's mind.

5. Practice: Using repetition and callbacks effectively requires practice. Rehearse your presentation and experiment with different techniques to find what works best for you.

By using repetition and callbacks effectively, you can create a memorable and impactful presentation that reinforces your key themes and messages.

USE SENSORY DETAILS TO IMMERSE YOUR AUDIENCE IN THE STORY:

As Mia walked down the narrow street, the savory aroma of fresh baked bread wafted through the air, instantly making her mouth water. She followed the scent until she came across a quaint bakery, its windows filled with rows of flaky croissants and colorful macarons. The bell chimed as she opened the door and a cozy warmth enveloped her, mingling with the fragrant scent of butter and sugar that seemed to dance in the air. Mia's eyes widened in delight as she watched the baker meticulously shaping a loaf of dough and sliding it into the oven with practiced ease. She could almost feel the heat from the oven and the soft, pillowy texture of the freshly baked bread. The sound of the crisp crust cracking under her teeth was music to her ears. She closed her eyes and savored the delicious moment, feeling like she had found a little slice of heaven in that charming bakery.

PRACTICE AND REHEARSE YOUR STORY TO REFINE YOUR DELIVERY AND IMPROVE YOUR PERFORMANCE:

Here are tips on how to practice and rehearse your story to refine your delivery and improve your performance:

1. Record yourself: One of the most effective ways to improve your storytelling performance is by recording yourself and listening to it. This will enable you to identify areas where you need to improve and track your progress.

2. Practice with a timer: Set a timer and practice speaking your story within a specific time frame. This will help you refine your pacing and ensure you stay within your allotted time for your presentation.

3. Seek feedback: Practice your story in front of friends, family members or colleagues and ask for their feedback. This will enable you to identify areas where you need to improve and refine your delivery.

4. Memorize key points: While it's essential to have a natural delivery, memorizing key points or quotes can help you stay focused and make sure you miss no critical elements of your story.

5. Rehearse in front of a mirror: Stand in front of a mirror and practice speaking your story. This will help you focus on your body language, eye contact and overall delivery.

Practicing and rehearsing your story is key to refining your delivery and boosting your performance. Remember to seek feedback, record yourself and continue to make changes until you achieve your desired outcome.

USE YOUR OWN UNIQUE STYLE AND VOICE TO MAKE YOUR STORY MEMORABLE AND IMPACTFUL:

Once upon a time, in a land far, far away, there was a little girl with big dreams. She dreamed of flying through the clouds like a bird, of exploring unknown lands and of finding true love. And even though life was challenging and full of obstacles, she never stopped believing in herself. With every step she took and every breath she took, she became stronger and more determined. And in the end, she found everything she had dreamed of and more, because she had the courage to never give up on herself or on her dreams.

6

LEVERAGING EMOTIONAL APPEAL IN YOUR SPEECHES

UNDERSTANDING THE POWER OF EMOTIONS IN INFLUENCING AUDIENCES' PERCEPTIONS AND DECISIONS:

Emotions are powerful drivers of human behavior, and they play a crucial role in shaping audiences' perceptions and decisions. People are not always rational beings, and their responses are often driven by their emotions. When we see something that evokes negative emotions, our natural reaction is to avoid it. Conversely, when we feel positive emotions, we are more attracted and drawn toward it. This is why emotions are powerful tools for marketers and communicators.

Understandably, a well-executed emotional appeal can trigger viewers to empathize with the message, whether joyous or heart-rending. And by extension, such an emotional campaign can influence how the viewers perceive the brand, product, or service it advocates for. This is because the human brain processes emotional information differently from rational data. Unlike rational data, emotional information sparks excitement, generates memories, and stimulates action.

This has been acknowledged by advertisers, who have adopted aspects of emotional advertising in their marketing campaigns. For example, advertising for charities is usually emotional, with images of disheveled, starving kids or animals. Also, popular brands like Coca-Cola, Budweiser, and Google have successful campaigns every year because they target feelings of joy, love, and nostalgia.

Finally, for all audiences, the essential first step is to identify what emotions they associate with your message. With that knowledge, communicators can target the right buttons to evoke an emotional response. A compelling message that appeals to positive emotions, like joy or the opportunity to belong, has a higher likelihood of influencing an audience's perception of a brand or product positively.

IDENTIFYING THE KEY EMOTIONS THAT RESONATE WITH YOUR AUDIENCE AND ALIGNING YOUR MESSAGE WITH THEM:

Here are some general tips for identifying and aligning messages with audience emotions:

1. Research your audience: Before you craft your message or content, it's important to understand your target audience. Learn about their behavior, interests, and beliefs.

2. Analyze their behavior: Try to understand their online behavior and the content they engage with. An audience that shares and engages with funny content is likely to resonate with humor.

3. Choose the right emotions: Pick two to three emotions that best fit your audience persona. For example, if you're targeting young adults with an adventure travel package, the emotions of excitement, thrill, and freedom can be good choices.

4. Use language that resonates: Your choice of words can evoke certain emotions. Use a tone and language that reflects the emotions you want to evoke in your audience. This could be humorous, exciting, emotive or heartwarming.

5. Connect emotionally: Create a connection with your audience through shared experiences or beliefs. This will create empathy and connection which could result in increased engagement with your message.

Overall, it's important to remember that your message may resonate with different emotions for different audience segments, so conduct research and testing to ensure the message is received positively by the intended audience.

USING STORYTELLING TECHNIQUES TO EVOKE EMOTIONS AND CREATE A MORE ENGAGING SPEECH:

Once upon a time, there was a young girl named Lily who lived with her family in a small village. Lily was curious and adventurous, always eager to explore the world around her. One day, she heard about a beautiful garden at the edge of the forest. It was said the garden was truly magical, and whoever entered it would be granted one wish. Lily couldn't resist her curiosity and embarked on a journey to find the magical garden.

As she trekked through the dense forest, she encountered many obstacles. She had to maneuver around thorny bushes, cross treacherous streams, and avoid deadly creatures. After many days of wandering, she finally came upon the beautiful garden. The lush greenery, colorful flowers, and beautiful fountains were truly breathtaking.

Lily was in awe and felt her heart fill with hope and excitement. She bravely stepped forward and made her one wish - she wished for a life filled with happiness and love. Suddenly, the garden came alive, and the air was filled with beautiful music. A magical creature appeared before her and granted her wish.

Lily returned home, feeling fulfilled and grateful. She realized that true happiness comes from within and from the love of those around you.

Through the use of storytelling techniques, the audience can be quickly drawn into the narrative and feel the same emotions as Lily. By painting a vivid picture of the journey, she undertook, the obstacles she faced, and the final outcome of her wish, the speech becomes more engaging and memorable. The audience is transported to another time and place, and they can relate to Lily's desire for happiness and love. Storytelling is a powerful tool for creating a connection with the audience and evoking strong emotions that inspire action.

INCORPORATING METAPHORS, ANALOGIES, AND OTHER LINGUISTIC DEVICES TO INSPIRE EMOTIONAL RESPONSES:

Language is a powerful tool that can evoke various emotional responses within us. Metaphors, analogies, and other linguistic devices can create a profound impact on our thoughts and feelings. Effective use of these devices can inspire, educate, persuade and even change us.

Metaphors are a way to connect two seemingly unrelated things to create a deeper understanding of an idea. For example, describing a challenging problem as a mountain to be climbed can help people to visualize the journey ahead and feel empowered to overcome it. Similarly, describing love as a rose can evoke feelings of fragility and beauty, while also hinting at the thorns that may come with it.

Analogies are another powerful linguistic device that can inspire emotional responses. Comparing a complex issue with a puzzle that needs to be solved gives people a sense of accomplishment when they finally find the solution. Analogies can also add humor to a situation or create a memorable image in people's minds.

Other linguistic devices like alliteration, rhyme, and rhythm can make a message more memorable and impactful. Using these devices can create a strong emotional response in the reader, listener, or viewer. They are particularly effective in creative writing or advertising where the goal is to create a strong emotional connection between the audience and the brand.

Metaphor, analogy, and other linguistic devices can inspire, educate, persuade, and entertain. They are a powerful tool that can create a lasting impact on the people, emotions, and actions. As a writer, marketer, or communicator, it is vital to understand how to use these devices effectively to achieve a specific emotional response from the audience.

RECOGNIZING AND AVOIDING COMMON PITFALLS OF EMOTIONAL APPEAL, SUCH AS MANIPULATION & OVERUSE:

1. Be cautious of oversimplification: Emotional appeals may sometimes be too simplistic and avoid important complexities, limiting critical thinking.

2. Use credible sources: Over-reliance on emotional content can lead to manipulation, especially when using unverified sources. Always make sure the message communicates factual information.

3. Don't rely only on statistics: While statistics can be an important tool for engaging emotions, they need to be put in context, especially if it leads to fear-mongering or sensationalism.

4. Avoid exaggeration: Emotional appeals must avoid overstatements, overblown language, and senseless hyperbole that can seem manipulation.

5. Don't overdo it: Too much emotion can lead to a backlash, as people see the message as manipulative or dishonest. Applying moderation is key.

Finally, always remember that overuse of emotions in communication may lead to counterproductive results, including loss of credibility and rejection of the message. So, moderation, context, and information should remain the center of all emotional appeals.

BALANCING EMOTIONAL APPEAL WITH RATIONAL ARGUMENTATION TO CREATE A PERSUASIVE & CREDIBLE SPEECH:

For crafting a powerful and convincing speech, it is essential to balance emotional appeal and rational argumentation.

Emotional appeal can help establish a rapport with your audience and encourage them to connect with the topic at hand. However, relying only on emotions can often veer into manipulation or superficial appeals. When crafting a persuasive speech, it is crucial to back up your emotional appeals with factual evidence and logical arguments.

But a speech purely logical and rational can seem cold or unconvincing. Using emotional appeal effectively can create a sense of urgency or relevance to the topic for the audience. However, this should be done in a way that does not diminish the factual evidence or logical arguments being presented.

To balance emotional appeal and rational argumentation effectively, understand the needs and values of your audience. This can let you tailor your approach to what your audience is seeking, making sure your appeal resonates with them on an emotional level while providing a strong logical basis for your argument.

Ultimately, a persuasive and credible speech requires both emotional appeal and rational argumentation. By striking the right balance, you can create a compelling and impactful message that will resonate with your audience and lead them to action.

IMPLEMENTING STRATEGIES FOR DELIVERING EMOTIONAL SPEECHES WITH AUTHENTICITY & CONVICTION:

As a speaker, you want to make an emotional impact with your audience, delivering a message that will resonate with their hearts and minds. You want to be authentic and convincing, so your words come from a place of purpose and passion.

Here are strategies to help you deliver emotional speeches with authenticity and conviction:

1. Connect with your audience: before you even write, take the time to learn about your audience. Who are they? What do they care about? What are their concerns? Use this knowledge to personalize your speech and make it relevant to your audience.

2. Use vivid language: when you speak, use descriptive and emotive language that will help your audience connect with your message. Use metaphors and storytelling to bring your message to life.

3. Be vulnerable: being authentic means being vulnerable. Share your own experiences and emotions in your speech. Let your audience see your humanity and they will connect with you more deeply.

4. Practice, practice, practice: rehearse your speech in front of friends, colleagues, or even a mirror. This will help you perfect your delivery and make your emotions more genuine.

5. Believe in your message: the most effective speakers believe in their message. Believe in what you are saying, and your conviction will shine through.

6. Use effective body language: your body language can also help convey your emotions. Make eye contact with your audience, use hand gestures to emphasize key points, and vary your tone and pace to keep your speech engaging.

7. Use humor: humor can be an effective way to engage your audience and make your message more memorable. Use humor to connect with your audience and lighten the mood.

Remember, delivering an emotional speech is not about manipulating your audience's emotions, but about sharing your own feelings in an authentic and honest way. By using these strategies, you can deliver a powerful and meaningful message that will leave a lasting impact on your audience.

～

❦ 7 ❦
HOW TO USE STATISTICS TO STRENGTHEN YOUR ARGUMENT

INTRODUCTION TO THE IMPORTANCE OF USING STATISTICS IN PERSUASIVE WRITING & ARGUMENTATION:

As a society, we are continually bombarded with information from multiple sources. It is vital to distinguish facts from fiction when making arguments or presenting persuasive writing. Statistics, the branch of mathematics that deals with the collection, analysis, and interpretation of data, can be a powerful tool in helping to back up a writer's beliefs and opinions. By using relevant data, statistics can provide concrete evidence that can support a position, making arguments more convincing and persuasive. In this way, statistics play a crucial role in persuasive writing and argumentation, helping to make arguments more persuasive and convincing by giving them a factual and scientific basis. The importance of statistics in persuasive writing and argumentation cannot be overstated, as it lets a writer make a more compelling and convincing case by backing up their claims with data and evidence.

UNDERSTANDING DIFFERENT TYPES OF STATISTICS AND THEIR USES:

Statistics is a branch of mathematics that deals with the collection, interpretation, analysis, and presentation of data. Different types of statistics are used to extract information from data. Some of the common types of statistics include descriptive statistics, inferential statistics, and probability theory.

Descriptive Statistics:

Descriptive statistics are used to summarize and describe a dataset. Descriptive statistics include measures of central tendency, such as mean, median, and mode, measures of variability, such as range, variance, and standard deviation, and measures of shape, such as skewness and kurtosis. Descriptive statistics provide a way of understanding the data and can help identify patterns, trends, and outliers.

Inferential Statistics:

Inferential statistics are used to make inferences or predictions about a population based on a sample of data. Inferential statistics involve hypothesis testing and estimating parameters. Inferential statistics can determine if an observed difference or relationship between variables is statistically significant, meaning it is not likely due to chance.

Probability Theory:

Probability theory is a branch of mathematics that deals with the measurement of uncertainty. Probability theory is used to determine the likelihood of an event occurring based on the available information. The probability of an event ranges from 0 (impossible) to 1 (certain). Probability theory is used to predict outcomes where there is uncertainty, such as in games of chance, weather forecasting, and financial investments.

. . .

Understanding the different types of statistics is important for data analysis and decision-making. Descriptive statistics are helpful for summarizing and understanding data, inferential statistics are useful for making predictions and testing hypotheses, and probability theory is essential for dealing with uncertainty.

TIPS FOR FINDING AND EVALUATING STATISTICS FROM RELIABLE SOURCES:

Here are tips for finding and evaluating statistics from reliable sources:

1. Identify reliable sources: Look for data and statistics from reputable sources, such as government agencies, academic institutions, and well-known research organizations.

2. Check for the source's expertise: Assess the author or organization's expertise and qualifications to evaluate their credibility for producing the statistics or data.

3. Access primary sources: Primary sources are always preferred over secondary sources. Primary sources include original research studies, surveys, and experiments.

4. Check for relevance: Statistics should relate to your research or study. Check whether the data is recent or outdated and whether it applies to your specific population and research question.

. . .

5. Verify peer review status: Peer review status indicates that the research or data has been evaluated by experts in the same field, making it more reliable.

6. Evaluate sampling methods: Check the sampling methods used to collect the data, as it can influence the accuracy and reliability of the statistics.

7. Check for transparency: Verify whether the data sources, methods, and analyses are transparent and whether authors explain their limitations.

8. Use multiple sources: Cross-checking the reliability of multiple sources can help you ensure the data's validity and reliability.

By following these tips, you can find and evaluate statistics from reliable sources, making sure your research and studies based on trustworthy data.

WAYS TO INCORPORATE STATISTICS EFFECTIVELY INTO YOUR WRITING:

The following are general tips for incorporating statistics effectively into writing:

1. Start with a clear and concise explanation: Before presenting any statistical data, provide a brief introduction to your readers that defines the problem and explains the significance of the statistics you will present. Be clear and concise, as readers may become overwhelmed with complex terms and ideas.

. . .

2. Choose the right data: Select statistics that are relevant and reliable. It is also essential to provide proper attribution to your sources to ensure their accuracy and avoid plagiarism.

3. Use visual aids: Visual aids, such as graphs and charts, can help to make numerical data more accessible and easier to understand. Label and title each chart or graph properly and use colors that make the data easy to distinguish.

4. Include key takeaways: Following the presentation of statistical data, summarize the essential findings in a few key takeaways. This can help to reinforce the significance of your statistics and stimulate your readers' interest in your work.

5. Keep it simple: While incorporating statistics into your writing can be beneficial, overuse can lead to confusion or disinterest. Remember that readers may not be familiar with statistical terms, so use simple language and avoid jargon.

6. Highlight significance and relationships: Often, the most valuable insights from statistics come from identifying relationships and trends. Highlight these findings in your writing and provide context for their significance.

Incorporating statistics effectively into writing requires careful consideration of the data's relevance, accuracy, and presentation. By following these tips, writers can make numerical data more accessible and engaging while supporting their arguments with evidence-based reasoning.

STRATEGIES FOR AVOIDING COMMON STATISTICAL FALLACIES AND ERRORS:

Here are tactics to avoid common statistical fallacies and errors.

1. Understand the data: Before making any conclusions, it's critical to review the dataset and understand its limitations, such as missing values or outliers.

2. Check the source: Always verify the accuracy of the source, making sure the data is reliable and unbiased.

3. Define terms: Ensure that all terms and variables are well-defined, avoiding any ambiguity or confusion.

4. Choose appropriate statistical tests: Understand which statistical tests are appropriate for your data and experiments.

5. Avoid confirmation bias: Be open to alternative explanations and interpretations of the data.

6. Identify correlation vs. causation: Recognize that correlation differs from causation. Correlation only means two variables may be related; it does not mean one variable causes the other.

7. Beware of misleading visualizations: Ensure that any graphs or visual representations are clear and do not misrepresent the data or conclusions.

. . .

8. Seek peer review: Before publishing or presenting any findings, get input from others in the field for constructive feedback and critique.

By following these strategies, you can avoid falling into common statistical fallacies and errors and make more accurate and reliable conclusions.

EXAMPLES OF HOW STATISTICS CAN ENHANCE ARGUMENTS IN DIFFERENT CONTEXTS, FROM POLITICAL DEBATES TO SCIENTIFIC RESEARCH:

1. Political debates: During political debates, statistics can support their arguments. For example, a candidate can use statistical data to show that a certain policy has succeeded in other countries or that a particular demographic supports their stance on an issue. In this way, statistics can add credibility to the argument, making it more persuasive.

2. Scientific research: In scientific research, statistics play a vital role in analyzing data and drawing conclusions. Researchers use statistics to provide evidence that their hypothesis is true or false. For example, a researcher can use statistical analysis to show the effectiveness of a new drug treatment. Without statistics, research findings would lack legitimacy and be open to interpretation.

3. Business decision-making: In the business world, statistics are often used to make informed decisions. For example, market research can provide statistical data on customer preferences, letting companies decide based on the needs and wants of their customers. Additionally, statistics can analyze financial data, such as revenue, profits, and costs, which can inform business strategy.

· · ·

4. Social debates: In social debates, statistics can reveal patterns and trends. For example, a statistician can analyze crime data to identify patterns and trends in criminal behavior, which can inform law enforcement strategies. Additionally, social researchers can use statistics to identify disparities in healthcare outcomes among different racial or ethnic groups, providing evidence to support policy changes aimed at reducing these disparities.

5. Educational research: In education, statistics can analyze student performance data, identify areas of improvement, and inform teaching strategies. For example, a teacher can use statistical analysis to identify trends in student performance data, such as areas where students are struggling, which can inform instructional decisions. Additionally, educational researchers can use statistics to evaluate the effectiveness of specific interventions and programs aimed at improving student outcomes.

ETHICAL CONSIDERATIONS WHEN USING STATISTICS IN ARGUMENTATION:

Here are thoughts about ethical considerations when using statistics in argumentation.

In any argument or debate, statistics can be a powerful tool to support a viewpoint. However, the misuse or manipulation of those statistics can lead to false conclusions and unethical practices.

One of the most important ethical considerations when using statistics in argumentation is to make sure the data is represented accurately and honestly. This involves making sure the data is collected ethically, and that the methods used to analyze and interpret the data are sound. It also means avoiding manipulation of the data, such as cherry-picking results or using statistical techniques that may obscure or exaggerate the true nature of the data.

Another ethical consideration when using statistics in argumentation is to avoid making misleading claims or presenting data to be deceptive to the audience. This can include using statistics presented to be misinterpreted by the audience, or leaving out important information that could change the audience's perception of the data. It also means avoiding making claims not supported by the data, or if are not justified by the evidence.

Finally, it is important to consider the potential consequences of using statistics in argumentation. This includes considering the impact that the results may have on the audience or the wider community. For example, manipulating statistics to support a particular viewpoint may lead to policy decisions harmful to certain groups in society, or may undermine public trust in science and research.

Ethical considerations are important when using statistics in argumentation. By making sure data is collected and analyzed ethically and presented accurately and honestly, it is possible to use statistics to support arguments in a way that is informative and transparent. Ultimately, this can help to build trust, enhance understanding, and promote ethical decision-making.

$\sim$

❦ 8 ❧

BODY LANGUAGE AND NONVERBAL COMMUNICATION IN PERSUASIVE SPEAKING

THE IMPORTANCE OF BODY LANGUAGE IN PERSUASIVE SPEAKING:

Here is an explanation why body language is an essential part of persuasive speaking.

Communication is not just about the spoken word; it also involves nonverbal cues such as body language, facial expressions, and tone of voice. With persuasive speaking, body language plays a crucial role in delivering a convincing message effectively.

Body language can help speakers emphasize certain points and deliver the message with more authority. It can show confidence, enthusiasm, and sincerity, which are all essential for persuasive speaking.

For example, in a persuasive speech, using open and expansive gestures can convey a sense of openness and confidence, making the audience feel more comfortable with the speaker. But a speaker who hunches down and avoids eye contact might be perceived as nervous or insincere.

Another example is maintaining eye contact with the audience. It shows that the speaker is confident, interested, and attentive. It helps build trust with the audience, which is crucial in persuading them to act or accept the speaker's message.

Body language can also help the speaker to connect emotionally with the audience, making it easier to convey the intended message. A speaker who uses body language can create a connection with the audience, making them more receptive to the message.

Body language plays an integral role in persuasive speaking. It helps convey the message more effectively and build trust with the audience. Speakers should, therefore, pay attention to their body language and use open and confident gestures, maintain eye contact, and connect emotionally with their audience.

THE DIFFERENT TYPES OF BODY LANGUAGE AND HOW THEY IMPACT COMMUNICATION:

Body language is the nonverbal form of communication that plays a significant role in relaying messages and expressing emotions between individuals. It includes gestures, facial expressions, posture, eye contact, and tone of voice. Understanding the different types of body language and their impacts on communication can go a long way in enhancing communication.

Facial expressions

Facial expressions are an essential part of body language as they convey emotions, attitudes, and intentions. A smile can show happiness, acceptance, or agreement. Raised eyebrows can show surprise or curiosity, while a frown indicates sadness or disapproval. Facial expressions can build trust, rapport, and emotional connections between individuals.

Gestures

Gestures can enhance, complement, or even contradict verbal communication. For example, a nodding head indicates agreement, while shaking the head indicates disagreement. A pointed finger or hand gesture can show emphasis, direction, or urgency. Gestures can also regulate conversations, indicate emotions, and express various meanings.

Posture

Posture refers to the way a person carries themselves, including their standing or sitting position. It can show confidence, assertiveness, or submissiveness. Standing up straight and keeping eye contact will indicate confidence, while slouching down indicates insecurity or disinterest. Posture can affect how others perceive us and can convey different messages.

Eye contact

Eye contact is a crucial nonverbal communication tool that indicates interest, attentiveness, and respect. Looking directly into someone's eyes can signify honesty, trustworthiness, and connection. However, avoiding eye contact may show insecurity, guilt, or disinterest.

Tone of voice

Tone of voice is the way words are spoken - the intonation, rhythm, and emphasis placed on certain words. It can convey emotions, attitudes, moods, and intentions. A monotone voice can show boredom, while a high-pitched tone can show excitement. The tone can affect the overall message we want to communicate.

Understanding and effectively using body language can help people communicate more effectively, build relationships, and achieve mutual understanding. The different types of body language can convey powerful messages, but it's essential to use them correctly and in the right context to enhance communication.

HOW TO USE BODY LANGUAGE EFFECTIVELY TO ENHANCE YOUR MESSAGE

Body language is a powerful tool you can use to enhance your message and communicate more effectively with others. Research has shown that as much as 60-90% of our communication is nonverbal, so the way we use our bodies can be as important as the words we say. Here are tips for using body language effectively:

1. Be aware of your posture

Your posture can convey a lot about how you feel and your level of confidence. Stand up straight, keep your shoulders back, and your head up when you want to seem confident and in control.

2. Use gestures to emphasize your points

Gestures can be an effective way to emphasize important points or ideas. Keep them natural and not overdo it, however, or else you risk coming across as insincere or untrustworthy.

3. Make eye contact

Eye contact is crucial in building connections with others and conveying sincerity. When speaking with someone, maintain eye contact, but avoid staring them down or making them feel uncomfortable.

4. Use facial expressions to show emotion

Your face can be a powerful tool in communicating your emotions and feelings. Smile when appropriate, frown when discussing something sad or difficult, and try to show enthusiasm and excitement when discussing something that you are passionate about.

5. Be mindful of your body language during group conversations

When you are in a group setting, be mindful of your body language and how it is being perceived by others. Avoid crossing your arms or legs, which can signal defensiveness, and try to maintain an open and welcoming posture.

By using body language effectively, you can enhance your message, build stronger connections with others, and ultimately become a more effective communicator.

THE IMPACT OF NONVERBAL COMMUNICATION ON AUDIENCE PERCEPTION:

Nonverbal communication is the communication we all do but often overlook. It's the way we communicate without using words, such as facial expressions, body language, eye contact, and tone of voice. It is said that sometimes, our nonverbal messages convey more than what we verbally communicate.

There is a massive impact of nonverbal communication on audience perception. Nonverbal cues can enhance or detract from the verbal message, and sometimes, it might even change the message's meaning altogether. For example, the same message delivered with different expressions could be interpreted differently by two people.

Facial expressions play a significant role in audience perception. A speaker's face can reflect nervousness or confidence, interest, or boredom. Audience members look for facial cues to determine if the speaker is trustworthy and genuine. Maintaining eye contact with the audience not only shows confidence and sincerity but also helps the speaker connect with listeners emotionally.

Body language is another essential factor that affects audience perception. Posture, gestures, and movements can emphasize or distract from the spoken message. Audience members unconsciously read a speaker's body language and interpret their engagement, confidence, or authority.

The tone of voice is another part of nonverbal communication that affects audience perception. A monotone voice lacking warmth or enthusiasm will not hold the attention of the audience. But a voice with emotion and energy can arouse interest.

Nonverbal communication significantly affects audience perception. Speakers who can master nonverbal cues can enhance the audience's understanding and retention of the message, as well as establish a more meaningful connection with their audience. Nonverbal communication is an essential communication skill to master.

TIPS FOR UTILIZING NONVERBAL CUES TO CREATE A MORE PERSUASIVE MESSAGE:

Here are tips for using nonverbal cues to create a more persuasive message:

1. Eye contact: Maintaining eye contact with your audience or listener during a conversation, speech or presentation shows you are confident, trustworthy, and engaged with the topic. It also helps to build a connection and establishes a rapport.

2. Body posture: Your body posture, how you stand, and use of gestures play a significant role in conveying confidence and authority. Stand tall and avoid crossing your arms, which can make you look defensive, or slouching, which can make you seem disinterested.

3. Facial expressions: Smiling, nodding, and demonstrating appropriate expressions that align with your message or agenda can help you influence your audience positively. People are more likely to respond favorably to a speaker who seems approachable, friendly, and welcoming.

4. Vocal tone: The way you use your voice can also affect your persuasiveness. Mirroring the tone and rhythm of the person you are speaking to can help them feel more receptive, and using variations in tone and inflection can keep the listener engaged.

5. Use of space: Utilizing the physical space around you can also contribute to a persuasive message. Walking around can help captivate your audience, and placing objects or images that align with your message can reinforce it visually.

By incorporating these nonverbal cues, you can create a more persuasive message and engage your audience more effectively.

COMMON MISTAKES TO AVOID WHEN USING BODY LANGUAGE IN PERSUASIVE SPEAKING:

Using body language during a speech is a vital part of persuasive speaking. It can either enhance the message you're communicating or detract from it. As artificial intelligence (AI) continues to revolutionize human communication, here are common mistakes to avoid when using body language in persuasive speaking:

1. Forgetting the Importance of Eye Contact:

When talking to an audience, one common mistake is not making eye contact with the audience. By keeping eye contact, you will communicate sincerity, confidence, and interest. Lack of eye contact will undermine your message by making you seem insincere, indifferent, or nervous.

2. Failing to Use Gestures:

Gestures like pointing, waving, and nodding can help to reinforce your message, show enthusiasm, and engage the audience. But stilted and awkward gestures can distract, and the audience may find it hard to relate to the speaker.

3. Lack of Confidence:

Your body language can tell if you are confident or not. A speaker who stands stiffly with their arms by their sides, with their head lowered, communicates insecurity and nervousness. But a speaker who stands straight, makes eye contact, and uses confident hand gestures communicates self-assurance.

4. Being Too Animated and Distracting:

While using body language is essential, being too animated may make you appear over the top, causing your message to be lost to the audience. Find a balance between using gestures and maintaining composure.

5. Overdoing Body Language:

Too much of anything is poisonous. Overuse of body language can be a turnoff and distract your audience from the message. Use gestures that match your message, and don't overdo them to avoid being too distracting.

The purpose of using body language during a persuasive speech is to reinforce your message and present yourself in the best light possible. By eradicating these common mistakes, you can communicate effectively using body language to meet your goal of getting your message across to the audience.

THE ROLE OF CULTURAL AND GENDER DIFFERENCES IN INTERPRETING BODY LANGUAGE AND NONVERBAL CUES:

Body language and nonverbal cues are significant elements in human communication. They help in augmenting, contradicting, or emphasizing verbal messages. However, the interpretation of these nonverbal cues can be affected by cultural and gender differences.

Cultural and societal norms influence body language, facial expressions, and physical gestures. For example, in some cultures, maintaining eye contact with authority figures is considered a sign of respect, but in other cultures, it is seen as a sign of disrespect. Similarly, the way people express emotions through their facial expressions can differ significantly. For example, in some cultures, it is considered rude to show teeth while smiling, but in others, it is a sign of happiness.

Gender also plays a significant role in interpreting body language and nonverbal cues. Gender socialization varies across cultures, and people may display different nonverbal cues based on their gender. For example, men may show more dominant body language, such as standing with their feet apart and arms crossed, while women may show more submissive body language, such as crossing their legs or arms and leaning their heads down.

Interpreting nonverbal cues can differ based on the gender of the perceiver too. In general, women are more expressive of their emotions than men. Hence, men may interpret nonverbal cues as less significant or dismissive, while women may view them as critical.

Cultural and gender differences can significantly affect the interpretation of body language and nonverbal cues. It is crucial to be aware of these differences when working and interacting with people from diverse backgrounds. By doing so, we can prevent misunderstandings and improve communication.

❧ 9 ❧
BUILDING CREDIBILITY AND
TRUST WITH YOUR AUDIENCE

THE IMPORTANCE OF ESTABLISHING CREDIBILITY AND TRUST:

E stablishing credibility and trust is essential in building long-term relationships with others. It is the foundation of any successful interaction, whether it be personal or professional. When a sense of trust is present, it fosters open communication, promotes mutual respect, and allows for productive collaboration.

In business, building a trustworthy reputation is crucial for success. Customers and clients are more likely to do business with someone they trust and believe in. Salespeople who have established credibility are often viewed as experts in their field and are more likely to close deals.

In personal relationships, trust is equally important. Friends, family members, and romantic partners who display consistent honesty and reliability are more likely to develop deeper, more fulfilling relationships.

Without trust and credibility, relationships can quickly become strained and unproductive. It's difficult to repair damaged trust, and sometimes, it's impossible to regain. Once broken, it can take years to rebuild.

Establishing credibility and trust is vital in personal and professional relationships. It is the foundation on which healthy relationships are built and the key to long-lasting success.

STRATEGIES FOR BEING CONSISTENT AND TRANSPARENT WITH YOUR AUDIENCE:

1. Establish clear communication channels: To ensure consistency and transparency with your audience, it's important to establish clear communication channels they can use to reach you. This could include email, social media, phone, or even a dedicated chat app for your business. Have a process in place for responding to messages promptly and professionally.

2. Be honest and open: Your audience will appreciate honesty and openness, especially for sharing information about your business. If you make a mistake, own up to it and try to rectify the situation. Be transparent about your business practices and policies and provide information about your products and services.

3. Set clear expectations: Consistency is key to building trust with your audience. Set clear expectations for your audience about what they can expect from you. This could include posting new content regularly, responding to messages within a certain timeframe, or providing updates on new products or services.

4. Document your processes: To ensure consistency, it's important to have documented processes in place for your business activities. This could include your social media strategy, your customer service protocol, or your content creation process. This way, everyone involved in your business can follow the same processes and provide a consistent experience for your audience.

5. Measure and analyze: Measure and analyze the results of your communication and engagement with your audience. This will help you determine what's working and what's not, so you can adjust as needed. Use analytics tools to track metrics like engagement, reach, and conversion rates to get an accurate picture of how your audience is responding to your messaging.

HOW TO EFFECTIVELY COMMUNICATE YOUR EXPERTISE AND EXPERIENCE:

Communicating your expertise and experience is important to establish credibility and build trust with your audience or clients. Here are tips on how to do it effectively:

1. Identify your target audience: Determine who you are communicating with and their needs. This will help you tailor your message and use language that resonates with them.

2. Be confident but not arrogant: Confidently communicate your knowledge and experience but avoid coming across as self-absorbed or boastful. Be humble and focus on how you can help others.

3. Use relatable examples: Use stories and examples to illustrate your points and make your expertise real and relevant to your audience.

4. Speak in simple terms: Avoid using jargon or technical language that your audience may not understand. Speak in terms easy to follow and comprehend.

5. Show don't tell: Demonstrate your expertise and experience through concrete examples, accomplishments, or results. This can include case studies, projects, or reports that showcase your skills.

6. Listen actively: Effective communication is not just about what you say, but also how you listen. Be open and actively listen to your audience's concerns, questions, and feedback. This will help you tailor your message to meet their needs.

By following these tips, you can effectively communicate your expertise and experience to establish credibility and build trust with your audience.

THE IMPACT OF STORYTELLING AND RELATABLE CONTENT:

Storytelling and relatable content have a significant impact on our lives. It is through relatable content we can connect with others on a deeper level and understand their experiences. When we hear a story that resonates with us, we feel a sense of belonging and validation. This is because we are social creatures, and we thrive on connecting with others.

In the digital age, storytelling and relatable content have become essential tools for marketers and advertisers. Brands that can tell a story and create relatable content can connect with their audience and build loyalty. By creating content that speaks to the needs and desires of their audience, brands can forge deeper relationships and foster trust.

Another area where storytelling and relatable content are proving to be beneficial is in education. Teachers who use stories and relatable content to teach their students can make learning more engaging and memorable. This is because stories create an emotional connection that helps us remember important information.

Storytelling and relatable content can also support social causes and raise awareness about important issues. By creating content that tells the stories of people affected by social issues, we can help to promote understanding and drive change.

Storytelling and relatable content have a powerful impact on our personal lives, marketing strategies, education, and social causes. By creating and sharing compelling stories and relatable content, we can connect with others, build relationships, and inspire positive change.

WHY AUTHENTICITY IS KEY TO BUILDING TRUST:

Authenticity is key to building trust because people want to know that they can rely on what you say and do. When you are authentic, you are genuine and transparent in everything you do, which helps build trust with others. People are more likely to trust someone who is open and honest with them, and who doesn't hide behind a façade or pretend to be something they're not.

Authenticity helps build trust in several ways. First, when you are authentic, you show you are true to yourself and your values. This allows others to see that you are sincere, and that you can be trusted to do what you say you will do. Second, authenticity creates a sense of connection and relatability with others. When you are open and honest, people are more likely to feel comfortable around you and to see you as someone they can relate to.

Finally, authenticity helps build trust by creating a sense of consistency and dependability. When you are authentic, you are more likely to behave consistently over time, which helps others know what to expect from you. This predictability creates a sense of dependability, which informs trust.

Overall, authenticity is key to building trust because it creates a foundation of reliability, consistency, and dependability that helps others feel comfortable and secure in their relationship with you. When you are authentic, you show you can be trusted, and this can help build strong, lasting relationships built on mutual respect and trust.

TIPS FOR RESPONDING TO CRITICISM AND FEEDBACK IN A PROFESSIONAL MANNER:

1. Listen and understand: Listen attentively to the criticism given and try to understand the underlying message. Do not interrupt or become defensive, as this can show a lack of professionalism.

2. Take a moment to process: Take a moment to process the feedback and avoid reacting impulsively. Consider the validity of the feedback and how it may be an opportunity for professional growth.

3. Respond with gratitude: Be gracious in your response and express appreciation for the feedback. This shows you value feedback and will learn and improve.

4. Respond with empathy: Try to understand where the feedback is coming from and respond with empathy. This can help to diffuse any tension and show you are open to working toward a solution.

5. Take ownership: Take ownership of any mistakes or shortcomings pointed out. This shows you are accountable and willing to take corrective action.

6. Follow up: Follow up with the person who gave you the feedback to let them know how you plan to implement their suggestions. This shows you take feedback seriously and are committed to improving.

THE ROLE OF INTEGRITY AND ETHICS IN CREATING A TRUSTWORTHY BRAND:

As businesses compete for customers' attention, creating a trustworthy brand is critical to standing out in a crowded marketplace. Trustworthiness is built on a foundation of integrity and ethics, which play essential roles in shaping a brand's reputation.

Integrity is about aligning actions with values. In a brand context, it means being honest, transparent, and consistent in all interactions with customers, employees, and stakeholders. When a brand consistently shows integrity, it builds trust with its customers and earns a reputation for being authentic and reliable. This reputation can be strengthened through communication that shows the brand is committed to accountability, social responsibility, and finding ethical solutions to challenges.

Ethics are the principles that guide behavior in a situation. In business, ethical behavior means adhering to both the letter and the spirit of laws and regulations while also following a set of moral principles. This approach not only reduces legal risks but also fosters long-term trust among all stakeholders. Brands that focus on ethics understand that short-term gains at the expense of long-term relationships with customers and stakeholders are not sustainable.

Trustworthy brands that focus on integrity and ethics are driven by a culture of honesty, transparency, and accountability. Reputation is everything in the current marketplace, and a failure to focus on these values can quickly erode that reputation. Brands that consistently show integrity and ethics earn customers' loyalty and support for years to come.

The role of integrity and ethics in creating a trustworthy brand cannot be overstated. In a competitive market, customers often make buying decisions based on the perceived values of a brand. Focusing on integrity and ethics can help businesses establish a reputation for trustworthiness, which can lead to customer loyalty, increased sales, and long-term success.

~

10

RESPONDING TO OBJECTIONS AND COUNTERARGUMENTS

UNDERSTANDING THE IMPORTANCE OF ANTICIPATING AND RESPONDING TO OBJECTIONS & COUNTERARGUMENTS IN EFFECTIVE COMMUNICATION:

Effective communication involves not only presenting your ideas and arguments persuasively but also addressing and responding to objections and counterarguments that may arise. Expecting and addressing objections and counterarguments can significantly enhance the persuasiveness of your communication and increase your credibility as a communicator.

When you expect objections and counterarguments, it shows you have considered multiple perspectives and are open to feedback and criticism. It also shows you are confident in your own arguments and can defend them against potential criticisms.

By addressing objections and counterarguments directly, you can mitigate any potential backlash that may arise from your audience. This helps to build trust and rapport with your audience, who are more likely to be receptive to your ideas if they feel heard and valued.

Addressing objections and counterarguments strengthens your communication by fostering an atmosphere of open dialogue and critical thinking. By encouraging your audience to engage with your ideas critically, you can spark meaningful conversations and gain valuable feedback that can help you refine your arguments and communication style.

Expecting and responding to objections and counterarguments is an essential part of effective communication. When done well, it can increase your persuasiveness, enhance your credibility, and cultivate a culture of open dialogue and critical thinking.

IDENTIFYING COMMON OBJECTIONS AND COUNTERARGUMENTS THAT MAY ARISE IN DISCUSSIONS AND DEBATES, & UNDERSTANDING WHY THEY MAY BE RAISED:

When engaging in discussions and debates, there are common objections and counterarguments that may arise. Understand these objections and the reasoning behind them to effectively address them.

One common objection is the appeal to tradition. This argument suggests that something is true or should be continued simply because it has always been done that way. The counterargument to this is that just because something has been done a certain way in the past does not necessarily mean it is the best or most ethical option going forward.

Another objection often raised is the slippery slope argument. This argument suggests that if one action is taken, it will lead to negative consequences. The counterargument is that a slippery slope argument is not always valid and may be based on fear rather than facts.

A third objection is the ad hominem argument, which attacks the person making the argument rather than the argument itself. This is often used to discredit the person and avoid addressing the actual point being made. The counterargument to this is that attacking the person rather than the argument is an illogical and ineffective way to engage in a discussion or debate.

Additionally, some may raise objections based on their beliefs or experiences. Understanding these objections and finding common ground can help to move the discussion forward and find a solution that works for everyone involved.

Recognizing and understanding objections and counterarguments in discussions and debates is crucial for effectively addressing them and finding common ground. By doing so, the likelihood of finding a satisfactory solution is greatly increased.

DEVELOPING STRATEGIES FOR RESPONDING TO OBJECTIONS AND COUNTERARGUMENTS, SUCH AS ACKNOWLEDGING VALID POINTS AND PRESENTING ALTERNATIVE PERSPECTIVES:

As a business or sales professional, it is important to develop strategies for responding to objections and counterarguments from customers. Here are tips on how to acknowledge valid points and present alternative perspectives:

1. Listen carefully: When a customer raises an objection, listen carefully to what they are saying. Try to understand their perspective and the reasons behind their objection.

2. Acknowledge the objection: Always acknowledge the customer's objection and confirm their concerns. Let them know that you understand their perspective and appreciate their feedback.

3. Provide a different perspective: Once you have acknowledged the objection, provide an alternative perspective. For example, highlight the benefits of your product or service, or explain how it can address the customer's specific needs.

4. Be prepared with facts and data: It is important to have data and facts to support your counterarguments. This can help to build credibility and strengthen your position.

5. Use stories and examples: Stories and examples can be an effective way to illustrate your point and show the customer how your product or service has helped others in similar situations.

6. Stay calm and respectful: Even if the customer becomes emotional or confrontational in their objection, remain calm and respectful. Responding in a professional and courteous manner can help to de-escalate the situation and move toward a resolution.

Overall, responding to objections and counterarguments requires active listening, empathy, and clear communication. By acknowledging valid points and presenting alternative perspectives, you can build trust with your customers and ultimately close more sales.

AVOIDING COMMON PITFALLS WHEN RESPONDING TO OBJECTIONS AND COUNTERARGUMENTS:

When responding to objections and counterarguments, avoid common pitfalls that can derail the conversation and lead to misunderstandings. Some of these pitfalls include becoming defensive, dismissive, or antagonistic. Here are tips to help you navigate these challenges:

1. Listen actively: One of the most important things you can do when responding to objections and counterarguments is to listen actively. Pay attention to what the other person is saying and take time to understand their perspective. Avoid interrupting or dismissing their concerns, even if you disagree with them.

2. Be empathetic: Try to see the situation from the other person's viewpoint. Show empathy and understanding, even if you don't agree with their position. This can help build trust and encourage the other person to consider your perspective as well.

3. Stay calm and respectful: It's easy to become defensive or dismissive when someone challenges your position, but this response is unlikely to be productive. Instead, stay calm and respectful, even if you feel frustrated or angry. Remember that a respectful conversation can help you both learn and grow.

4. Avoid personal attacks: Attacking the other person is never a good strategy. It can make them defensive, shut down communication, and damage relationships. Instead, focus on the issue at hand and use facts, data, and evidence to support your position.

By avoiding these common pitfalls, you can have productive and respectful conversations, even when faced with objections and counterarguments. Remember to listen actively, show empathy, stay calm and respectful, and avoid personal attacks. With these strategies, you can build stronger relationships and find common ground with others.

BUILDING ON PREVIOUS ARGUMENTS AND EVIDENCE PRESENTED IN ORDER TO STRENGTHEN RESPONSES TO OBJECTIONS AND COUNTERARGUMENTS:

Building on earlier arguments and evidence is a crucial part of strengthening responses to objections and counterarguments. Revisit key points made earlier in the argument and reinforce them with more evidence and reasoning.

For example, if the initial argument is that climate change is caused by human activities, an objection might be that the climate has always gone through natural cycles of warming and cooling. In response, it would be important to repeat evidence from scientific studies that show human activities such as burning fossil fuels and deforestation are the primary drivers of climate change.

Building on earlier arguments can also involve expecting objections and addressing them in advance. This requires careful consideration of the possible counterarguments that opponents may use and providing evidence to refute each one.

Overall, building on earlier arguments and evidence helps to establish a strong foundation for an argument and makes it harder for opponents to refute. By doing so, it enhances the persuasiveness and credibility of the argument, making it more likely to convince others.

USING RHETORICAL TOOLS, SUCH AS ANALOGIES AND EXAMPLES, TO MAKE RESPONSES TO OBJECTIONS AND COUNTERARGUMENTS MORE PERSUASIVE:

Rhetorical tools, such as analogies and examples, are effective ways to make responses to objections and counterarguments more persuasive. Analogies can create a relatable comparison that makes difficult ideas more understandable. For example, if someone objects to the cost of a new car, you could use the analogy of a long-term investment, such as buying a house, to explain how the cost will be worth it, eventually.

Examples are another powerful rhetorical tool that can bolster an argument. By providing concrete examples, you can make a case more convincing and harder to refute. For example, if someone counters your point on the importance of renewable energy by saying it's too expensive, you can cite examples of companies and countries that have successfully implemented renewable energy sources and saved money, eventually.

Analogies and examples can help your audience see your argument from a fresh perspective, which can be especially helpful when dealing with tough or polarizing issues. These rhetorical tools can help to shine new light on an issue, or highlight parts of the topic that may have been overlooked.

Analogies and examples are powerful tools that can improve the persuasiveness of responses to objections and counterarguments. By using these rhetorical devices, you can help your audience better understand your point, and you can make a stronger case for your position.

ADDRESSING ETHICAL CONSIDERATIONS WHEN RESPONDING TO OBJECTIONS AND COUNTERARGUMENTS:

Addressing ethical considerations in response to objections and counterarguments is crucial in maintaining a respectful and productive dialogue. It is essential to avoid ad hominem attacks, which are personal attacks on the opponent rather than responding to their argument. This behavior can be harmful and unproductive, as it detracts from the substance of the debate and degrades the conversation.

It is also important to avoid misrepresenting opposing views, which means it's essential to accurately represent the opposing argument without twisting their words or cherry-picking pieces to bolster your argument. This behavior is unethical as it creates a strawman and misrepresents a person's argument, making it easy to weaken their stance falsely.

When responding to objections and counterarguments, consider the principles of respect, honesty, and fairness. It's essential to listen to the opposing arguments carefully, and respond in a way that is respectful of the other person's views, truthful, and fair. This approach helps to foster a productive, constructive conversation that can lead to a better understanding of the other person's perspective.

If you encounter an opposing view you feel is disrespectful or unethical, use your language to steer the conversation back to a respectful, productive, and ethical path. Using ethical principles in responding to counterarguments, you make sure your conversation is aligned with your values and maintains a respectful tone.

11

ETHICAL CONSIDERATIONS IN PERSUASIVE SPEAKING

THE IMPORTANCE OF CONSIDERING ETHICAL IMPLICATIONS WHEN ENGAGING IN PERSUASIVE SPEAKING:

Persuasive speaking is a powerful tool that can persuade an audience to agree with the speaker's viewpoint or to take a particular action. However, persuasive speaking can also manipulate, deceive, or harm others. So it is essential to consider the ethical implications when engaging in persuasive speaking.

Ethics are the principles and values that guide our behavior in relation to what is right and wrong. In persuasive speaking, ethics are crucial because they help make sure the speaker does not use their power of persuasion to deceive, manipulate, or harm others. Instead, ethical behavior enables the speaker to use their persuasive skills to provide information, educate, and persuade others in a truthful and respectful manner.

Ethical considerations in persuasive speaking include the speaker's intention, the message they deliver, and the impact it has on the audience. The speaker should be transparent about their motives and avoid using deceptive tactics to persuade the audience. They should also ensure the accuracy of the information they provide and avoid using emotional appeals that exploit the audience's vulnerabilities.

Another ethical consideration is the impact of the message on the audience. The speaker should consider the potential consequences of the message they deliver, especially where it may cause harm or negatively affect vulnerable groups of people. Ethical speakers are mindful of the potential impact of their message on the audience and try to mitigate any negative consequences.

Ethical considerations are crucial when engaging in persuasive speaking. Being mindful of ethical principles makes sure speakers use their persuasive skills in positive ways that benefit the audience rather than causing harm or deception. By being ethical in their approach, speakers can build trust, credibility, and respect with their audience, ultimately leading to more significant and sustainable positive results.

THE POTENTIAL HARM THAT CAN BE CAUSED BY UNETHICAL PERSUASION:

Unethical persuasion refers to manipulating and influencing individuals to take actions or make decisions not in their best interests. It can cause severe harm to both the persuader and the persuaded. The potential harm that can be caused by unethical persuasion includes:

1. Loss of autonomy: Unethical persuasion undermines the ability of an individual to make their own choices and decisions. This can cause a loss of autonomy and self-determination.

2. Emotional distress: When individuals are coerced and manipulated into making decisions, they may experience negative emotions such as anxiety, depression, and guilt. This can lead to emotional distress and mental health issues.

3. Financial loss: Unethical persuasion may also cause financial loss as people are influenced to buy products or invest in schemes that do not align with their best interests.

4. Damage to relationships: Unethical persuasion can also damage relationships as it involves deceptive and manipulative tactics. This can result in mistrust and breakdown of relationships.

5. Legal and regulatory implications: In extreme cases, unethical persuasion can result in legal and regulatory implications. Using unethical tactics to influence individuals to make decisions can lead to lawsuits, fines, or even criminal charges.

The potential harm caused by unethical persuasion is significant and can have serious consequences for both the persuader and the persuaded. Businesses and individuals must focus on ethical persuasion to protect themselves and their stakeholders from harm.

FACTORS TO CONSIDER WHEN DETERMINING WHAT CONSTITUTES ETHICAL PERSUASION:

When determining what constitutes ethical persuasion, several factors must be considered to make sure the persuader is acting in a morally responsible and respectful way toward the audience. These factors include:

1. Audience Vulnerability: Persuaders must know the level of vulnerability of their audience. Vulnerability can come in various forms, such as emotional, mental, or physical, and it can affect the way the audience perceives the message. Ethical persuaders must avoid taking advantage of their audience's vulnerability and instead, approach them with kindness and empathy.

2. Truthfulness: The persuader must always be truthful in their communication. Persuasion involves changing someone's beliefs or actions; however, it should never be done through deception or misleading tactics. All claims and promises made should be backed up by evidence, and the persuader should avoid exaggerating or withholding important information.

3. Respect for Autonomy: Ethical persuaders must respect their audience's autonomy, so they should never try to force or manipulate their audience into making a decision. Instead, they should provide neutral and fair information to help the audience make an informed decision. Persuaders should also respect the audience's right to refuse or accept the message.

4. Use of Evidence: The persuader must use credible and reliable evidence when presenting their message to the audience. Evidence should be accurate, relevant, and presented in a way that the audience can easily comprehend. The persuader should also be able to explain the evidence if the audience has questions.

5. Transparency: The persuader must be transparent about their intentions and motives. They should reveal any conflicts of interest or biases that may influence their message. This will help the audience evaluate the message's credibility and make an informed decision.

Ethical persuasion requires the persuader to have empathy for their audience, be truthful, respect their autonomy, use credible evidence, and be transparent about their intentions. By considering these factors, the persuader can create persuasive messages that are not only effective but also ethical.

STRATEGIES FOR ENSURING ETHICAL PERSUASION:

Ethical persuasion is the act of trying to convince someone to adopt a particular belief or act in a certain way, without coercing or manipulating them. Make sure persuasion is ethical to maintain trust and credibility, and to avoid taking advantage of vulnerable individuals. Here are strategies for ensuring ethical persuasion:

1. Use evidence-based claims: When persuading someone, it is important to present credible evidence to support your argument. Evidence can be in the form of research studies, statistics, factual information, or expert opinion. Use credible sources to back up your claims and make sure the evidence is up-to-date and relevant.

2. Avoid emotional manipulation: Emotions are a powerful tool with persuasion, but it is essential to avoid manipulating others through fear, guilt, or other strong emotions. Instead, appeal to reason, logic, and intellect when presenting your arguments.

3. Be transparent about motives and biases: Be transparent about your motives when persuading someone, especially if you have a personal interest or motive in the outcome. Avoid hiding your biases or interests and be upfront with the individual about your intentions.

4. Engage in active listening: To effectively persuade someone, engage in active listening. Pay attention to the individual's concerns, listen to their perspectives, and respond respectfully to any disagreements they may have.

5. Encourage critical thinking: Encouraging critical thinking can help individuals evaluate their arguments and make informed decisions. Ask open-ended questions and encourage the individual to ask questions and seek more information.

Ethical persuasion requires using credible evidence-based claims, avoiding emotional manipulation, being transparent about motives, engaging in active listening and encouraging critical thinking skills. By adhering to these strategies, it is possible to engage in ethical persuasion and build trust and credibility with others.

ETHICAL CONSIDERATIONS WHEN USING PERSUASIVE LANGUAGE:

Using persuasive language can be a powerful tool to get others to follow your ideas or beliefs. However, be mindful of ethical considerations when using persuasive language. Here are key considerations:

1. Avoid hate speech: Using language that denigrates certain groups of people is not only unethical, but it can also be illegal. Hate speech includes language that is derogatory, insulting or intimidating toward individuals or groups because of their race, gender, religion, sexual orientation, disability, or any other characteristic.

2. Use inclusive language: Persuasive language should be inclusive and avoid excluding any group of people. For example, using the pronouns "he" or "she" might exclude people who identify as non-binary. Using "they" instead can show you are accommodating all people, despite their gender identity.

3. Respect cultural differences: Different cultures have different communication styles, and what is persuasive in one culture might not be persuasive in another. Understand and respect these differences so you can use persuasive language that is appropriate and effective.

4. Be honest and truthful: Persuasive language should not involve lying or misleading people. Making false claims, omitting important information, or exaggerating your argument can be unethical and can damage your credibility.

Overall, ethical considerations when using persuasive language involve treating all people with respect and dignity, avoiding harmful language, being truthful and honest, and understanding cultural differences.

THE ETHICS OF TARGETING VULNERABLE POPULATIONS:

Marketing and advertising play an important role in today's world, but it is crucial to ensure ethical considerations when targeting vulnerable populations, such as children or the elderly. These groups are often susceptible to exploitation, and exercise sensitivity and caution when promoting products or services to them.

Children are especially vulnerable to various marketing techniques due to their limited understanding of the world and the impact of their actions. Advertisers often use cartoon characters, bright colors, and catchy jingles to attract children's attention, which can manipulate their choices and beliefs. They cannot make informed decisions without guidance, and it is vital to recognize that directly targeting them is not ethical. Marketers should not take advantage of their age to induce them to buy products, and regulatory measures need to be in place to prevent this exploitation.

Similarly, the elderly, too, can be vulnerable targets for certain advertising techniques. With their limited cognitive abilities and potential health problems, they may be more prone to being misled by false marketing claims, leading to adverse effects on their health and financial stability. For example, some marketers may use scare tactics to promote health supplements or medication, which can harm an elderly person's already delicate state of mind. So, it is crucial to be extra cautious and ensure these groups are not exploited.

To address these issues, strict guidelines for marketers and advertisers should be put in place. These should include considerations toward the psychological and physical health of children and the elderly. Advertisements should not be misleading, and claims made should be factual and legitimate. It is also essential to make sure advertisements are placed in channels that will not cause undue distress to these groups.

Targeting vulnerable populations through manipulative marketing techniques is not only unethical but also can have severe consequences. It is imperative to exercise sensitivity and caution when promoting products or services to children and the elderly. Appropriate measures must be taken to prevent the exploitation of these groups, protect their well-being, and maintain the ethical standards of marketing and advertising.

THE ROLE OF ETHICS CODES AND GUIDELINES IN REGULATING PERSUASIVE SPEAKING AND ENSURING THAT PRACTITIONERS ARE HELD ACCOUNTABLE FOR THEIR ACTIONS:

Ethics codes and guidelines play a significant role in regulating persuasive speaking and making sure practitioners are held accountable for their actions. Persuasive speaking involves presenting arguments to influence the opinions, attitudes, and behaviors of others to achieve specific goals. It requires a high level of ethical standards to make sure the information presented is truthful, reliable, and unbiased.

Ethics codes and guidelines provide a framework for ethical behavior in persuasive speaking. They outline the principles and values that practitioners in this field should adhere to, such as honesty, transparency, respect for others' opinions, and avoidance of manipulation or coercion. These codes and guidelines are important because they create a standard for the ethical conduct of practitioners, helping them to avoid ethical and legal violations.

Ethics codes and guidelines also help to set the boundaries for persuasive speaking. They provide guidance on what is acceptable and what is not, helping practitioners to avoid crossing the line into unethical behavior. So practitioners who follow these codes and guidelines are more likely to build trust with their audience and establish a positive reputation.

Besides, ethics codes and guidelines provide a mechanism for holding practitioners accountable for their actions. They provide a way of imposing sanctions or consequences on those who violate ethical standards. Sanctions may include revocation of professional licenses, termination of contracts, or even legal action. So practitioners aware of these ethical standards are more likely to act responsibly and avoid unethical behavior.

Ethics codes and guidelines play a vital role in regulating persuasive speaking and making sure practitioners are held accountable for their actions. They provide a framework for ethical behavior, set boundaries, and impose consequences for ethical violations. They contribute to the integrity of the profession, the effectiveness of communication, and the trust and confidence of the audience.

∾

CONCLUSION:

Persuasion is an essential skill for authors and speakers looking to make an impact on their audiences. Whether you're trying to sell a product, convince someone to adopt a new idea, or inspire them to act, the ability to persuade others is vital.

Throughout this book, we have explored the many facets of persuasion and provided practical advice on how to use them effectively. From understanding the structure of persuasion to leveraging emotional appeal, building credibility, and responding to objections, we have covered all the crucial elements that go into a persuasive speech or presentation.

We began by examining the structure of persuasion and how it's used to guide the development of a persuasive speech. We then delved into the psychology of persuasion, exploring the cognitive and emotional factors that influence decision-making. We also looked at how to craft a compelling speech outline and how to use rhetorical devices to enhance the persuasive impact of your speech.

We then moved on to discuss the power of storytelling in persuasive speaking, exploring how stories can create an emotional connection with the audience. We also examined how to leverage emotional appeal in your speeches and how to use statistics to strengthen your argument.

In Chapter Eight, we explored the role of body language and nonverbal communication in persuasive speaking. We discussed how to use body language to convey confidence and authority, and how to make sure your nonverbal cues follow your verbal message.

We then moved on to discuss how to build credibility and trust with your audience, examining the importance of establishing common ground and showing expertise. Finally, we looked at how to respond to objections and counterarguments, and how to handle ethical considerations in persuasive speaking.

The power of persuasion is an essential tool for authors and speakers looking to affect their audiences. By understanding the structure of persuasion, leveraging emotional appeal, and building credibility, you can create persuasive speeches that inspire action and change. With the practical advice and tips provided in this book, you have all the tools you need to become a more effective and persuasive speaker.

∼

ABOUT THE AUTHOR

Rae A. Stonehouse is a Canadian born author & speaker.

His professional career as a Registered Nurse working predominantly in psychiatry/mental health, has spanned four decades.

Rae has embraced the principal of CANI (Constant and Never-ending Improvement) as promoted by thought leaders such as Tony Robbins and brings that philosophy to each of his publications and presentations.

Rae has dedicated the latter segment of his journey through life to overcoming his personal inhibitions. As a 29+ year member of Toastmasters International he has systematically built his self-confidence and communicating ability.

He is passionate about sharing his lessons with his readers and listeners.

His publications thus far are of the self-help, self-improvement genre and systematically offer valuable sage advice on a specific topic.

His writing style can be described as being conversational. As an author Rae strives to have a one-to-one conversation with each of his readers, very much like having your own personal self-development coach.

Rae is known for having a wry sense of humor that features in his publications. To learn more about Rae A. Stonehouse, **visit The Wonderful World of Rae Stonehouse** at https://raestonehouse.com

Facebook: https://www.facebook.com/raestonehouse.aws

Twitter: https://twitter.com/raestonehouse

ALSO, BY RAE A. STONEHOUSE

Visit https://liveforexcellence.store/ for a selection of personal/professional self-development books by Rae A. Stonehouse.

If you have found this book to be helpful, please leave us a warm review wherever you purchased it.